P9-ELW-504

Windows on the River Neva

OTHER BOOKS BY PAUL GRABBE

MINUTE STORIES OF THE OPERA (1932)
with Paul Nordoff

WE CALL IT HUMAN NATURE (1939)
with Gardner Murphy

THE STORY OF 100 SYMPHONIC FAVORITES (1940)

OUTDOORS WITH THE CAMERA (1941)
with Joseph E. Sherman

STORY OF ORCHESTRAL MUSIC AND ITS TIMES (1942)

Windows on the River Neva

A MEMOIR
BY

Paul Grabbe

POMERICA PRESS LIMITED
New York

Copyright © 1977 by Paul Grabbe

All rights reserved, including the right to reproduce this book or parts thereof in any form except for the inclusion of brief quotations in a review.

Library of Congress Catalog Card No. 77-84876
ISBN: 0-918732-03-4

Manufactured in the United States of America

To Beatrice
from Pavlik

CONTENTS

LIST OF ILLUSTRATIONS

Following page 50

12. Uncle Sasha—Alexander Nikolayevich Bezak, Mother's oldest brother. (1910)

13. Uncle Kolya—Nicolai Nikolayevich Bezak, Mother's youngest brother with author and Nils in ballroom of St. Petersburg apartment. (1905)

14. Peasant women after church service. Village simpleton is in foreground, right. (1908)

Following page 146

15. Mother wearing pearl necklace, only valuable saved after the Revolution. (1903)

16. Father in field uniform as commander of Konvoy. (1915)

17. Author, aged thirteen, in uniform of Corps des Pages. (1915)

18. Grand Duchess Anastasia, the Tsar's youngest daughter, on the Imperial yacht *Standart*. (1912)

19. The Empress and daughters on board the Imperial yacht with Court Minister Count V. B. Fredericks. (1912)

20. The Empress with Father at Mogilev. (1916)

21. The Tsar relaxes near Mogilev six months before the Revolution. With him are three of his daughters and members of his retinue. Left to right: Grand Duchess Olga, Countess A. Hendrikov, lady-in-waiting, Grand Duchess Marie. Behind her, Grand Duchess Anastasia. Colonel A.A. Mordvinov, aide-de-camp, kneels behind the Tsar. At far right is the

author's father taking picture with "squeeze bulb" cable release. (1916)

22. *Princess Margaret*, the British minelayer on which the Grabbe family escaped from Riga. (*Photo:* Imperial War Museum, London)

23. The author, age seventeen, after rescue. (1919)

24. The epergne presented by refugees to Captain H. H. Smyth of *Princess Margaret*.

25. The Tsar looking from the window of the Imperial train. (1916)

Following page 181

Map showing route of the Grabbe Family's escape from Russia.

Windows on the River Neva

1

TO THE MANNER BORN

We stood, Mother and I, on the grass in the Congregational cemetery at Kent, Connecticut. Facing us across the open grave was a minister reading prayers. "Ashes to ashes and dust to dust," I heard him say, and then Father's coffin was lowered into the grave. The year was 1947, mid-March; the ground was only recently unfrozen.

"I'm glad you chose this spot," Mother said. "These birch trees remind me of Russia." She moved a few paces away, reluctant to leave. Her gaze followed the minister as he hurried to his car.

The undertaker, who had been standing by discreetly, approached us. "Do you want a cement slab over the coffin?"

Something in me wanted to cry out: "Yes, yes, by all means!" Instead, I looked at him. "What for?" I asked.

"To keep the earth from settling, you know. The type of soil here . . ."

"Well, I guess, if you think it is a good idea . . ."

I tried to sound indifferent, to keep my voice steady. I felt like running away, bolting. I didn't feel secure even with

Father in his grave. He might yet reach out and somehow get at me. I would have agreed to two slabs instead of one—to keep Father safely underground.

Why?

What had Father done to me? He was a big man, but not threatening nor malevolent. I was a big man, too—at forty-five. Age did not seem to matter. Although I knew Father was dead, I still felt something close to panic. It was not only my horror in the presence of a corpse; there was something else, too. I was afraid of my father, dead or alive. Why? Psychoanalysis had given me some clues. A cousin had provided another. As a child in St. Petersburg, I liked to sit on Mother's lap and play with her hair, Cousin Ella told me. Father disapproved. Yes, dimly I remember. Actually, it is only this year that I was able to recall one such instance. Recall? Or imagine?

Alone in a strange city, Brussels, I woke up in the night. Seemingly out of nowhere came the memory.

I see myself, a child of three, sitting on Mother's lap and fondling her lustrous, black hair. The door opens. Father comes in. He has been gone, and now he is back. He strides toward Mother and lifts me off her lap. With a passing kiss he sets me down on the floor. Then he takes Mother in his arms and kisses her while I stand there disconsolate and helpless, just looking.

"Why don't you go to your room and play!" Father commands.

I turn and leave, but as I close the door behind me, I can't resist the temptation to peep through the keyhole. Unexpectedly, Father opens the door. "You still here?" he demands angrily. He glares. The look on his face chills me. I turn and run.

St. Petersburg early in the century was a special world. My part of it must have been quite special, too. Father was a Cossack general, an imposing man, with his uniforms and handsome blond mustache. He was also a man of affairs. As military aide during the last years of the monarchy, he had easy access to the Tsar. When I was thirteen, he sent me to the Corps des Pages, an exclusive military school. He had gone there himself and had enrolled me at birth. He must have hoped that I, too, would become a general. And, from his point of view, why not?

As a child I took my family's position and material well-being for granted. It seemed natural to be fussed over by nurses and governesses. Until I went to military school I rarely saw any other children except my older brothers, Nils and Georges. That may be why a nurse or a tutor became so important to me. They served as playmates.

There was one nurse to whom, I am told, I was devoted. Her name was Pasha. I have a snapshot of her here. It shows a little woman with pretty blond hair and a determined manner. When Mother asked her to care for me on a trip to the French Riviera, she had to refuse. She couldn't bear to leave Russia, she said, even for a short time. When we left without her, I felt bereft.

After we arrived in Cannes, in protest I refused to eat desserts. Baffled, Mother summoned my favorite waiter at the Elysée Palace Hotel, where we were staying, to talk me into eating a slice of cake.

"*Ce délicieux gâteau,*" he pleaded. "Perhaps an orange or a tangerine?"

"It is unnatural for a child not to want desserts," Mother told my new Latvian nurse. But no. I shook my head. No, no, no, I gestured vehemently, though I loved desserts.

I missed Pasha. Never again could I give my affection to any other nurse or governess.

Parting from Pasha was hard. Much harder would be parting from Russia later on.

2

A BABY NO MORE

Late one night I was awakened by Father shaking my shoulder. We were in the compartment of a train en route somewhere. The train was standing still. Father was looking down at me and saying: "Get up, Pavlik. Get up. We have to leave this train. It isn't going any farther." I was reluctant to get up, and I wondered what was happening.

Father helped me put on my bathrobe. It was dark red, woolly, and warm. "There was an accident," he said. "We are transferring to another train. Mother and Nils are already there, and our luggage is with them." Then Father hoisted me on his shoulder and walked with me along the passageway. He opened the door of the train and went down some steps. Outside, the moon was shining and I could see quite far. It wasn't very cold. With me still on his shoulder Father made his way along the tracks. He walked past the locomotive, which was emitting sparks and making frightening hissing sounds. The train had stopped in a field, and other passengers were walking along the tracks.

Soon we came alongside some other railroad cars and
Father carried me up the steps and into a compartment like
the one we had left. "Here we are," he said, lowering me into
the berth. Then he tucked me in. "Sleep well." I caught a
glimpse of Mother looking at me through the door before I fell
asleep.

Next day we arrived in Cannes. I gathered from what
Mother said that something of which she disapproved was
happening at home in St. Petersburg and she wanted to get
us away. I later learned that we had left the capital—the year
was 1905—in order to escape the riots, strikes, and insurrec-
tions that threatened revolution. Since Father's military duties
required him to be on the Riviera, Mother decided that she
would go there, too, and stay until things quieted down in
Russia.

Father, then a colonel in the Guard Cossacks, was stationed
in Cannes as aide-de-camp of Grand Duke Mikhail
Nikolayevich, the Tsar's great uncle who had been field marshal of the Russian army. Father had come to know him
through his own father during a campaign in the Caucasus
when the grand duke was viceroy there. Later he had been
invited by the Grand Duke's sons, Aleksander and Sergei
Mikhailovich, to go with them to the Far East. Father's socia-
bility made him a pleasant companion. On this trip Father
had met the Tsarevich, who later became Tsar Nicholas II.

"In 1890," he says in his memoirs,

the Tsarevich undertook a voyage on the *Pamyat Azova* [Memory of
the Azov Battle] to the Far East and after a visit to India he came to
Ceylon for a two-week stay. At that time I was accompanying the
Grand Dukes Aleksander and Sergei Mikhailovich on their travels
aboard the yacht *Tamara*.

On the same day [that the Tsarevich reached Ceylon] the *Tamara*
came into Colombo and we spent the two weeks with the Tsarevich.

After ten days of official receptions and sightseeing tours, the Tsaverich declared that he wanted to spend the remaining four days without any official functions. He spent almost this entire time with us on the yacht *Tamara* and in walks [on shore]. Here the Tsarevich recognized me and showed that he was well disposed towards me.

Years later, the old grand duke remembered his sons' friend as an amiable young man and asked for his services as aide-de-camp. Father accepted the assignment at once. He was to stay in the post twelve years—1897–1909, from before I was born until I was nearly eight.

The Grand Duke's residence was at the capital, but he stayed part of the year in his country estate. One day he had a stroke. On doctor's orders he had to leave Russia for a warmer climate. He chose Cannes as his new residence, and Father had to go along.

The change raised problems for our family. With Father on the Riviera, Mother was left alone in St. Petersburg. Her upbringing had not prepared her very well to cope with a household and children all by herself. And Father had only short periods of leave to spend at home with us. Yet, what could be done about it? The pattern of life in his world precluded any other choice. Offered a plum, one took it. So Father was relieved when the family came to spend the troubled winter of 1905 near him on the Riviera, away from Russia.

Another Russian family, the Saburovs, were also passing the winter in our hotel. One day Mother decided to call on them, and she took me along. They had two boys about my age. When we went to call, both boys were on the floor, absorbed in some sort of game with an electric train. I wanted to join the game, but they said no. They wouldn't let me play with their train. I thought this wasn't right and said so. They still refused. To settle the argument their mother said to them, "Show him some of your other toys." Turning to Mother, she added something about my hair. "Isn't it about time?" I heard her say. Later that afternoon we said good-bye and left.

During this call I was dressed as usual in skirts and had long, curly hair. It was the way well-to-do little boys my age were supposed to look. Customarily, at the age of three or four, they were given a crew cut; short trousers were substituted for the skirts.

On the morning following our visit to the Saburovs, the hotel barber appeared in my room. He said he had instructions to cut off my curls. I refused to submit and asked for Mother. My Latvian nurse said Mother was out shopping. That very morning she had said I was old enough to have short hair. I couldn't believe it. I protested. The nurse held me firmly in the chair while the barber went snip, snip, snip. I yelled and kicked, but nothing helped. A little later, I watched forlornly as the maid swept up my beautiful red ringlets. Just then Mother returned. She brought me candy. I refused it. I would not even talk to anyone. Still later in the day, dressed in the short pants and jacket Mother had bought for me, I wandered alone among the palm trees in the hotel garden. I felt sad. I wanted to share my pain with someone. There was no one around, not even Nils. He had gone to the beach.

The next day, perhaps to make me feel better, Mother took Nils and me to a local theater. There was a matinee performance of Jules Verne's *Around the World in Eighty Days*. The first act seemed to go well enough, but in the second act the travelers were attacked by a band of Indians. There was sudden gunfire—bang, bang, bang—and a commotion on stage. Terrified by the loud detonations, I burst into tears. "Don't cry," Mother said. "It's only make believe." But I couldn't stop crying. The tears kept streaming down my cheeks, and I had to be taken back to the hotel before the end of the performance.

A month later came news that the disorders in Russia were under control. Soon after that, Father took us to the railroad station, and we were on our way home to St. Petersburg.

3

HOMECOMING

Returning to St. Petersburg by night train after trips abroad or summers in the country was always a joy. I liked to wake up early, stretch myself out in the comfortable berth, and savor the sensation of being whisked through space—the swaying of the railroad car, the rumbling of the train as it sped over the miles. When dawn came, I would reach for the window shade, raise it halfway, and peer out. In the fall, a typically bleak, northern landscape would meet my gaze. Marshes alternated with patches of leafless trees under a heavy sky. Abruptly the trees would end, and we would be racing past sodden fields that reached as far as one could see. A desolate landscape! Desolate, but so familiar. To me the marshes and the fields were a cheering sight. They meant that I was coming home.

Soon the train would reach the Nikolayevsky Station. Mother would take Nils and me by the hand and walk us along the platform to the exit. A carriage would be waiting. (A few years later it would be a car.) We would be driven

11

along the Nevsky Prospect, across the Fontanka Canal, and on toward our apartment at 26 Mokhovaya Street. Another five minutes and we would be home. Nils and I would race through all the rooms, making sure that everything was still the same as when we left. We would throw open cupboard doors, rediscover old toys, call to each other excitedly.

The neighborhood in which we lived was affluent and quiet. The street was only two blocks long. A tall policeman stood at the intersection. Nils and I named him Pyotr Arsenich. We waved a greeting to him whenever we went by. Directly across the street, there was a small chapel. It had a faded blue facade and narrow windows outlined in gold. An ikon was embedded in the wall over the entrance. As a child I liked to sit by the window of our playroom and watch the people who came to pray. I knew them by their clothes: shopkeepers, servants, factory hands (there was an iron foundry nearby), women with kerchiefs on their heads, and many others. Some hesitated on the threshold and crossed themselves before going inside. Occasionally a man would walk up the street, pause to take a bottle out of his pocket, and then, as I watched closely, hit the neck of the bottle against the stone wall to break it off. He would then empty the bottle in several long gulps. I thought at first that he was drinking water and was afraid the jagged glass would cut his mouth. One of the servants explained to me: the man was not drinking water; he was drinking vodka.

I wondered how this old chapel happened to be on our street, wedged between two larger buildings. No one in our household seemed to know. One day I overheard Mother say that she so wished the chapel could be torn down; it attracted undesirable people.

My bedroom windows opened on a courtyard. As a small boy of six or seven, I used to watch everything that went on below: the handyman—*dvornik*—chasing a stray dog or arguing with the knife grinder; the scullery maid, Vasilisa, hurrying across the yard. I had mixed feelings about Vasilisa. With peasantlike directness, she could be very blunt. I once accidentally dropped a coin into her dishpan and asked her to get it out for me. She gave me a disapproving look and said, "You dropped it in; you get it out. Nothing is in there to bite you." I knew she meant it, so I fished the coin out of the greasy dishwater.

Looking down at the yard, I also could see our cook, Danila, on his way to market. Sometimes he left early in the morning before I woke up. When he came back, he waved up at me and I waved back. Then, choosing the right moment, I would sneak into the kitchen to see him. I was not supposed to go into that part of the house. I wanted to hear Danila talk about his life, especially about his hobby, horse racing. He was always so friendly. I liked Danila.

From my bedroom window I sometimes caught a glimpse of a chimney sweep up on our roof. He lowered a brush down a chimney, brought it up, and lowered it again. He did not seem quite real; it was almost as if he had jumped right out of one of my storybooks and up on the roof. He was covered all over with black soot, even his face.

Directly below us on the first floor lived one of Mother's brothers, a bachelor who spent part of each year in Paris. He was a scholar, Mother explained to us; his field was French civilization. But to my brother Nils and me, he was plain Uncle Kolya, a tall man with a dark mustache who brought us fascinating toys at Christmas: huge teddy bears, electric trains, and once even a carousel in which Nils and I went round and round. *"On takoy dobryak!"*—Such a kind man!—Mother would say tenderly.

Poor Uncle Kolya! Soon after the Bolshevik takeover, he was arrested at the English Club while playing bridge. As he was being led away, he was picked off the street by an angry mob, thrown into the canal, and stoned to death. He was my favorite uncle.

4

26 MOKHOVAYA STREET

Our home in St. Petersburg was at 26 Mokhovaya Street. It is still there today, and it looks just as it did in my childhood, unchanged from the outside. Other emigré Russians may be glad to know that the Soviet government has left intact the dwellings in the center of the city. Apparently, quite a number, like our home, survived the siege of Leningrad. Recently, a Russian friend who lives in Paris not only visited his former home at 16 Mokhovaya Street; he was invited to tea by one of its present occupants.

When I think of my childhood home at 26 Mokhovaya Street, I think of our playroom and Nils playing the piano. I see the huge teddy bear in one corner, the carousel in another. Spread out on the floor, the tracks for my trains. I used to squat for hours trying to make two trains run simultaneously in opposite directions without colliding.

I think of Nils's multicolored maps on all four walls. I think of Nils himself. He was four years older than I. I hear him playing Schubert. He played a lot, but seldom touched the

14

grand piano in the ballroom except when Mother asked him to perform for guests. He hated playing for people who had no interest in music. But Mother usually got her way. She liked to show him off.

"It's easier to play than argue," he once told me.

In the playroom Nils had a special audience for his music: our pet turtle. I can still hear the thud, thud, thud it made as it waddled across the floor. It usually came out of hiding when Nils began to play and went directly under the piano, where it sat motionless. Once a dowager came to call on Mother and mistook Turtle for a footstool. To Mother's great amusement, the lady gasped when Turtle moved away. After that, Turtle was confined to our quarters.

Our canary also liked Nils's music. With the first note, it jumped up on its perch, cocked its head, and began to sing. Its gay song carried right through the closed doors into the next room.

This adjoining room was called the *prokhodnaya*—the passing-through room. We had to cross it to reach other parts of the apartment. A rather sizable room it was. At first glance it suggested a gymnasium. And no wonder. Along its walls were various kinds of athletic equipment: parallel bars, a ladder, and a pole for climbing. There was also a trapeze. Father was partial to gymnastics. In his youth he had excelled in sports, especially figure skating and horseback riding.

When we were very small, our lunches were served to us on an oval table in the *prokhodnaya*. A governess or tutor ate with us. During these meals we sometimes heard the muffled sounds of hammering and sawing, of carts unloading in the yard, and of unfamiliar voices shouting back and forth. We hardly noticed any of these sounds, but as we grew older we came to understand they had to do with one of Father's major interests—construction, the modernization of houses, including the one in which we had our apartment.

Few people within Father's circle of acquaintance were aware of this activity, and those who knew thought of it merely as an avocation. To the majority he was primarily a military man. This view of him was strengthened not only by his eye-catching uniform, but by his impressive military career. Though still in his mid-forties, he was a colonel and aide-de-camp to Grand Duke Mikhail Nikolayevich, patriarch of the Romanov family. As everybody knew, Father was destined to go still higher. But in reality, his main interest was in construction. Within the limitations imposed by his military career, he gave himself to this activity with relish.

When Father was home on leave, he spent much of his leisure time in his study examining blueprints and scribbling figures on a pad. Sometimes I watched him from the divan in the corner of the room. I was allowed to sit there on the Bokhara rug if I kept quiet.

Once Father took Nils and me to a building site. He pointed out what various workers were doing. He seemed to know everybody.

"How is Dunya these days?" he asked the foreman.

"Much better, Your Excellency," the foreman answered, pleased that Father remembered his wife's name.

We could see Father enjoyed talking to the men. I was beginning to realize that he had a faculty for getting on with people. He was a very human person. It hurt that he couldn't be around more to share this quality with us. Maybe that's why I was a little jealous of those construction workers.

One day he told us that in his youth he had wanted to go into the construction field, perhaps become an engineer. It hadn't come about, though. His father had gambled away not only what little money he had but his wife's fortune as well. And so he had a hard time educating his children. Everybody in the family looked to the rich maternal grandmother for support. Father did, too. He counted on her to finance his schooling. But Countess Elizaveta Alekseyevna Orlova-Denisova had her own ideas about what Father's career should be. When he expressed his wish to become an engineer, she would not hear of it.

"No!" she said firmly. "I won't allow it. You must join the Guard Cossacks, the regiment in which my husband started his career."

Recalling this scene, Father described his grandmother as imperious. Her manner, he said, discouraged argument. In her eyes, only two careers were suitable for a young man of good family and standing: diplomacy or a commission in a regiment of the Guards. And since there was no other source of money anywhere in sight, he yielded to her wishes.

Here I might pause to say a word about my great grandmother's background. It helps explain what made her such a formidable person. She was the granddaughter of a fabulous merchant, Savva Yakovlevich Yakovlev-Sobakin, who came from nowhere to push a fish cart on the streets of Moscow. Soon he had built a chain of liquor stores, and then proceeded to corner the customs concession in the capital. Linen factories and gold mines followed. A robber baron of his time, he bought his way into the nobility with a loan to Peter III. To mollify Catherine the Great, who didn't like his methods, he built a church and made a huge donation to her favorite charity. His son, understandably, dropped the Sobakin from the name. *Sobakin* in Russian means "doglike."

If her mother's father was a legendary character, Countess Orlova-Denisova's own father was no less remarkable. Aleksei Petrovich Nikitin, a member of the lesser nobility, was an orphan educated by Catherine the Great. As colonel of artillery at age thirty-six, he commanded the Raievski Redoubt at the Battle of Borodino. Though he was wounded in both legs, he and his battery held back Napoleon's advancing forces long enough to give Kutuzov's army a chance to regroup. For this deed he was officially declared a Hero of the Napoleonic War. Not only is this exploit described by Tolstoy, but every cinema version of *War and Peace* features it. Nikitin went on to gain further honors for which he was made a hereditary count. It is not generally realized these days that many titles of nobility trace back to some outstanding achievement like Nikitin's. He is an ancestor of whom I have reason to be proud.

Although the dowager countess refused to sanction an engineering career, it would seem to have been her intention to include Father in her will. She had even made an appointment with her lawyer for that purpose and was on her way to his office to sign the necessary papers. Alas, she was accompanied by her son who was at that time her sole heir. When they arrived at their destination, he reached to help her out of the carriage, saying, "The weather is good today, isn't it?"

"I think it's bad," she answered and paused to look at the sky.

"But I think it's really good," he insisted.

"And I say it's bad," she declared raising her voice.

"Really, *Maman*, it's good."

"Well, if you think it is so good, then why don't you stay out in it for a while?" She turned to the coachman. "Kusma!" she ordered. "Drive home."

And so the new document wasn't signed after all. Within a few days, the countess fell ill and died, and her son remained her only heir.

When this blow came, Father had already graduated from the Corps des Pages and had joined the Cossack regiment favored by his grandmother. At twenty-eight he married Mother. When he discovered that her dowry included several old city properties, his interest in construction was revived. As they were, the houses were unprofitable, but Father saw in them a vast potential. Here was an opportunity to try his hand at remodeling to bring an income. Soon he realized that what the city needed was not additional housing for the rich, but modern apartments for the rapidly growing sector of middle-income workers. He was one of the first in St. Petersburg to act on this insight. His pioneering effort eventually paid off. On his fiftieth birthday, four months after the start of World War I, he was a millionaire.

In making over the house we lived in at 26 Mokhovaya Street, Father created a thirty-room apartment for us on the second floor of what had been a six-story Baroque-style stone mansion. This apartment, comfortable and spacious though it was, seemed modest in comparison with some of the homes of families of greater affluence. Several mansions in our own neighborhood made this fact clear.

I remember in particular a town house just up the street to which I was taken every Sunday afternoon for dancing lessons. The house belonged to the Tolstoys. They had two children: a boy my age, Seryozha; and a girl, Dalechka, who was a little awkward and rather shy. The afternoon dancing class was customary in many homes. And were those Sunday afternoons exciting! After the dancing and refreshments, we scattered throughout the house in a wild game of hide-and-seek.

I always looked forward to these occasions. To me the house seemed enormous, glamorous. There was the thrill of the unknown about the games we played. Rampaging through the four-story mansion gave endless opportunities for exploration. Discovery followed discovery—of silent, empty rooms (whose occupant, a maiden aunt, was said to be away); of dark, concealed back stairs, which for some reason ran only from the third to the fourth floor; of unexpected and mysteri- -ous passageways . . .

There's another reason why I looked forward to those Sunday afternoons. They offered me an opportunity to play with other children. Such an opportunity did not come often. Within my parents' milieu, it was customary for children to play only with siblings and cousins, governesses and tutors.

And even at 26 Mokhovaya Street we were limited in our contacts. Actually, our U-shaped apartment was divided into three separate worlds, each opening on a different side of an inner courtyard. Father had planned the apartment that way. Although these worlds were adjacent to one another in the layout, each led its own existence.

At one end of the U were the pantry, kitchen, and quarters for the menservants. Here lived Danila, the cook; his two assistants; Yegor, the butler; a footman; Father's orderly; and the chauffeur, Vlasyuk. I knew something about their lives. I liked to linger in the pantry and talk to them.

Among the servants, Yegor was top man. Appropriately formal in demeanor, he seemed to me remote and cold. During short family absences he was left in charge of the household. It was through him that Mother learned of any problems affecting the staff. He also was the one who kept her current bottle of Château d'Yquem locked up and guarded her Huntley and Palmer gingersnaps. I, too, liked these cookies, but was not supposed to have any. They came from England, I was told, and were expensive. Whenever I tried to filch one, I usually failed. Yegor was vigilant and hard to circumvent. I didn't like him.

After the evening meal, the servants all withdrew to their own quarters. Unless specially summoned, they did not reappear until the next morning. Theirs was a world quite separate from ours.

In the center of the U lived Mother and Father, each with a bedroom, bathroom, and study. They were secluded from the rest of the household by intervening living, dining, and guest rooms. Because they had their own separate entrance and separate stairs, I had only a vague idea of their daily comings and goings. Nor did I know if they had callers and, if so, who they were.

In that middle area was also the ballroom. On two of its walls, facing each other, were enormous mirrors in white frames. Under one of the mirrors stood the grand piano partly covered by a red silk throw. There were draperies at the windows, a large, bronze chandelier, and very little furniture—only a line of delicate white chairs.

The ballroom was used mainly for children's parties. Just before Christmas a huge fir tree was set up in the middle of the room, its top a little to one side of the chandelier. Nils and I together with our governesses or tutors spent many hours decorating the tree with Christmas ornaments, gingerbread men, and little baskets filled with raisins and nuts. We also fastened to the branches small candle holders, each containing a brightly colored candle. Several cousins and a few other children, such as Dalechka and Seryozha, were usually invited to the annual Christmas party. The presents were arranged on small tables around the ballroom and then hidden under white tablecloths. Not until Yegor had lighted the candles on the tree and the children had been allowed to enter the room were the tablecloths removed and the presents distributed. Uncle Kolya's was always my favorite gift.

Every spring the ballroom was used for children's recitals organized by our piano teacher, Anna Drozdoff. As I seldom practiced, I dreaded these occasions. Anyhow, Nils was always the star performer.

There were still other uses for the ballroom, though dancing was not one of them. I never saw anyone dancing there except the *polotyory*—two men who came once a month to polish the floor. *Polotyory* means floor rubbers, and that's exactly what they were. After the wax was spread on the floor, each man attached a brush to his right foot and the pair moved along rhythmically, side by side, with their hands clasped behind their heads for better balance. After each stroke of the brush, they jerked their bodies sideways in a little dancelike movement. In this way they covered the entire area. I liked to watch them. When they were through, the floor glistened.

The children's quarters—our world—was at the opposite end of the apartment from the servants' quarters, across the courtyard. It was inhabited by Nils and me, our governesses or tutors, and three maids: One of the maids, Emilia, an Estonian, was Mother's lady's maid. As in the servants' part of the house, the children's section had its own bathroom and anteroom leading to a separate entrance and stairs. That anteroom marked the end of our domain. At that point, an invisible line separated us from our parents' world. We, the children, were not supposed to venture beyond that line unless properly attired and on our best behavior. But the regulation was not strictly enforced. To insist on it, in my parents' eyes, would have seemed too rigidly Germanic. The implicit constraint was there, nonetheless.

All told, our apartment housed some twenty people. To feed this establishment cost fifteen rubles a day, equivalent at the time to seven dollars and fifty cents.

When the food bill went up steeply, we knew that Danila had lost at the races or again taken to the bottle. Arguments followed, and recriminations. Then everything went on as before, until the next lapse. There was never any thought of parting with Danila. His father and grandfather had been cooks in our family. As a boy he was sent to France to study cooking and learned to combine Russian and French cuisine. He was proud of his skill. During the last week of Lent, to make fasting—which we observed in principle—more bearable, he tried especially hard to serve delicious food. Every day after dinner he conferred with Mother in her study on the next day's menu.

Sometimes I overheard these conversations as I stood concealed behind a curtain at the door of Mother's room. In this way, when I was about eight, I learned that the servants' food was not the same as ours. Theirs was simpler and it cost less. This information surprised me. Why should their food be different? Mother explained we had a food budget and had to stay within it. The servants' food was every bit as nourishing as ours, she said. I did not know what budget meant and could say nothing. I was too young to cope with Mother, who usually closed all arguments by saying that we did not have much money.

Although I took our style of life for granted, I thought my parents must be pressed for money—they made so much of small economies. Even the Tsar, Father liked to tell us, put out the lights when he left the room. Every fall when I was fitted for Nils's outgrown clothes, I was reminded of the need to save. As neither Nils nor I received a regular allowance, we had to haggle with Mother every time we needed money for a toy, a record, a book. The situation was demoralizing. It tempted me to help myself—to candy, small change, anything desirable that was within reach. I pried open closets and bureau drawers. On occasion I even borrowed from the servants.

Once at Christmas when the presents were being handed out, Uncle Sasha, Mother's oldest brother, gave me a five-ruble gold piece. He never got around to actually buying presents for anybody, but I knew there was more where that gold piece came from. Instead of thanking him, I said, "Uncle Sasha, please give me another five rubles." He looked startled, but fetched another gold coin from his pocket. Later Mother scolded me. "If you had saved that gold piece he gave you last year," she said, "you wouldn't have had to ask him now for more."

Save! Save! Don't spend! Put aside! Economize! These admonitions still ring in my ears. Not until my early teens did I realize that my family was really quite well off. Then I felt I had been misled.

Now I see that Mother's tendency to hoard wine and chocolate, her parsimonious habits in general, may have been caused by early insecurity. And a parent's gift of a gold thimble set with sapphires and diamonds was no compensation for a lack of love.

As for Father, he must have found material possessions important when he was a boy. With little means, it would have been hard to keep up standards and live in the manner of a Guards officer, especially on his trip to the Far East with the grand dukes. He held on even to trinkets—watches, locks, and other gadgets that he kept in his bureau drawer. Occasionally he allowed me to see his treasures. I couldn't touch—only look. To a small boy, even looking without touching can be a thrill.

One day he gave me a watch. "It's broken," he said, "but you might like to play with it." I was delighted, took it to my room, and tinkered with it until it started to run again. I rushed back to show Father I had made it work. "Good," he said as he took the watch and locked it up again with his other trinkets. I ran, wide-eyed, to Mother. Her reaction was not helpful. She reasoned that Father had probably intended not to give me a watch, but to give me a toy. According to this logic, when it started to run it ceased to be a toy and again became Father's watch.

As I heard Mother's words, some critical faculty in me came alive. "What Mother says doesn't make sense," I inwardly exclaimed.

Later, I became aware that my parents were inconsistent in other ways, too, notably about money. They were constantly reminding me that money is important, that money matters should not be taken lightly nor handled carelessly. At the same time, they brought me up never to mention money in a

social situation, certainly never to speak of the cost of anything. To do so was bad taste, they said. Bargaining was vul-
gar. Merchants were a questionable lot, whose aim in life
avowedly was to make money, an unworthy goal. It took me
years to realize that such views are irreconcilable.

5

THE BEZAK SYNDROME

"I tell you," Uncle Kolya would exclaim, "our government is paralyzed! Morally bankrupt! It should be pouring millions into rural education. The peasants must be taught to read and . . ."

"No, no! I don't agree," Uncle Sasha would interrupt, spearing his fork into the breast of chicken on his plate. "Not peasant education! These peasants, these *muziks*, I tell you, they're brutes! *Skoty*! No better than ordinary cattle. They can't be educated."

Such an exchange was typical. Mother's brothers showed little caution when they came to dinner. The tenor of their talk was both irreverent and unrestrained. I found their conversation fascinating.

Father was seldom present when my uncles stayed for dinner. Whether he felt he couldn't cope with them or whether their outspoken criticism of the government made him uneasy, I don't know. Certainly he must have thought them irresponsible—people of whom you must be wary lest they damage your career. I felt differently.

Uncle Sasha was the more indiscreet of my two unmarried uncles. Now I realize that he lacked social conscience. And he was arrogant. He did not hesitate to say whatever came into his head. He could afford such self-indulgence, for Mother's family had ample means.

My grandfather, Nikolai Aleksandrovich Bezak, had risen to high rank in the civil service under Alexander III to become minister of post and telegraph. My grandmother, Maria Feodorovna Bezak, born Louginina, was the only daughter of a landowner whose holdings included thousands of acres of woodland in the Upper Volga. Her brother, Vladimir Feodorovich Louginin, had distinguished himself as a chemist. He established at Moscow University the first Russian themodynamics laboratory.

When I think of the Bezaks, apart from the Louginins, I think of distinct family characteristics, which include tenacity and organizing ability. Also in the syndrome is a quick intelligence, honed perhaps by challenge. Mother's great-great-grandfather, Christian Bezak, a Lutheran, had these attributes.

The Bezaks did not originate in Russia. A leading bio graphical source traces them to Lusatia and gives the name as *Bezatsky*, that of an old Slavic family. Uncle Sasha looked into earlier antecedents and found the *de Besacks* were French Huguenots from Toulouse who took refuge in Austria-Hungary. A branch of the family found its way to Anhalt, Lusatia. There the *Russian Biographical Dictionary* picks up the family history.

The first ancestor to go to Russia was Mother's great-great-grandfather, Christian. A professor of philosophy at the University of Leipzig, he came to teach at the invitation of Catherine the Great. He Russianized the name to Bezak and soon had learned the language so well that he wrote several books. Over the years he rose in the civil service; on becoming College Councillor, he attained hereditary noble privileges.

Mother's grandfather, Aleksander Pavlovich Bezak, had the same need to excel. Handsome in an arrogant way, he rose from artillery officer to chief of staff of the artillery. Then, as governor general of Samara and Orenburg, he became a key figure in Russia's expansion into western Turkestan. After a period in the senate, he became governor general of Southwestern Russia. In Kiev he introduced peasant reforms of considerable importance and put through a railroad connecting Kiev with Moscow.

It is interesting to observe how the Bezak strain has asserted itself through the years, though not always constructively. I have particularly in mind Mother's oldest brother, Uncle Sasha—Aleksander Nikolayevich Bezak. Tenacity in his case turned to eccentricity; and intelligence, misapplied, became irresponsibility. Though brilliant, Uncle Sasha was coldly self-centered. When he laughed, he laughed drily; when he smiled, he did so with a look of disdain. His conversation was rapid, his inflection impatient, and he spoke in a high-pitched voice alternating between Russian and French using both with polished precision. What was most notable about him was that he was an eccentric on a grand scale, such as the world no longer produces. He had gone to the University of St. Petersburg, graduated with honors, and had served for a time as an officer in the prestigious Chevalier Garde.

But travel was his real occupation; he almost made it a way of life. Twice a year without fail he set off from the Capital, always on the fifteenth of the month, with his itinerary planned to the smallest detail. What is more, he let nothing get in the way of his journeys to far-off continents. When he was ordered by his commanding officer to be present at the annual regimental parade attended by the Tsar, he preferred to resign his commission rather than adjust his itinerary. For the opening of the opera season in St. Petersburg, however, he always got back in time.

Once in Kenya he was told he could not go directly to Guinea. He spread out a map, drew a line across Equatorial Africa, and said that's the way he'd go. And he did. How did he proceed? I was never told. He probably had read *Across Africa*, Verney Cameron's 1877 account of his pioneering journey. I don't even know whether he carried a gun with him. At the turn of the century, the only feasible way to cross Equatorial Africa from Lake Tanganyika would have been via canoe on the Congo River. Certainly it must have taken courage, if not foolhardy daring, an aberration of Bezak ability.

When something happened to interfere with his travel schedule, Uncle Sasha adjusted accordingly. Approaching Greece one time—perhaps on his way back from Africa—he found he was late for a train connection. Unperturbed, he rented a locomotive to catch up, taking a leaf, perhaps, from Jules Verne. When the curtain rose on the first act of *A Life for the Tsar* at the Imperial Marinsky Theatre, there was Uncle Sasha in his accustomed seat: front row, third from center, right.

To make sure he got the theatre tickets he wanted, Sasha employed a man who did nothing but stand in line to buy them. I don't know what this man did when Uncle Sasha was, say, in the Sandwich Islands. I suppose if I had asked him, he would have replied impatiently, "How should I know? Never gave it a thought."

Also employed by Uncle Sasha was an Englishman, one John Kirby, who traveled around the world with him. Mr. Kirby's duties consisted of packing the suitcases and providing companionship. He was also charged with keeping a record of the type, make, and number of each locomotive used en route. When the train happened to be pulled by a locomotive already on the list, the occasion called for champagne.

Mr. Kirby had other duties. While Uncle Sasha stayed in his steamship cabin or hotel suite, the Englishman was delegated to socialize with the ladies they chanced to meet on their travels and to report back to Uncle Sasha on his conquests. How do I know? Mother talked rather naively about it. Today we might look on Uncle Sasha as neurotic and his behavior as compulsive and sexually repressed. What was apparent to everyone at the time was that he was determined to do exactly as he pleased.

Another of Uncle Sasha's eccentricities related to the Russian Orthodox Church. When he was in St. Petersburg, he attended services in the darkly resplendent Kazan Cathedral; but it seems he was motivated not so much by faith as by the desire to catch one of the bishops in a mistake. It so happened that he knew every detail of the service. He not only pointed out errors to the abashed church dignitary; he also delighted in telling others. Such behavior can only be seen as decadent.

During the Revolution, he managed, through the help of his brother Fedya, to escape from Russia, and he made his way penniless to southern France. At that time someone suggested to Thomas Cook that Uncle Sasha's experience as a traveler might be invaluable in planning complicated itineraries. When Thomas Cook offered Uncle Sasha the job, he at once turned it down, preferring a hand-to-mouth existence. He would not, as he put it, "sell" his travel experiences. For several years he lived on in Nice and managed somehow—proud though pathetic. A while ago I visited his grave in the Cimetière de la Caucade on a hill overlooking the Mediterranean.

Mother's second brother, my Uncle Kolya—Nikolai

Nikolayevich Bezak—was different from Uncle Sasha, a more complex personality and much more human. Although he, too, had his peculiarities, he was less neurotic, less withdrawn. Everyone used to talk about his sharp tongue, though I can only remember his friendliness. He was a tall, thin, distinguished-looking man with a courtly manner. His apartment was in the same building as ours was, directly under Nils and me.

I recall the occasion—I must have been ten or eleven—when Nils and I ran into him on the stairs as he was about to enter his apartment. "Well, how are you today?" he greeted us with genial warmth. "Come in and tell me what you're up to." I had never been in Uncle Kolya's apartment before, and I was curious to see what it was like. We followed him into his study. I was but vaguely aware of the furniture, the paintings on the wall, the books, the thickly opulent Persian rug. What drew my attention was a picture in a silver frame on his desk. I walked right up to it. I wondered who the pretty young woman in the photograph was, but I was too shy to ask.

With Nils as with me, Uncle Kolya was the kindly uncle, warm and endearing. But he was not so with others. He had a reputation for cutting people down if he didn't like them or thought them stupid. At one point he joined the Russian civil service, became special assistant to the secretary of the senate. What he found there disillusioned him, and he resigned. After he left the government, he took up his earlier scholarly studies in French civilization. His interest in history he shared with his colleague at the Imperial Historical Society, Grand Duke Nikolai Mikhailovich, a liberal so outspoken in his criticism of the regime that the Tsar confined him to his estate. No wonder Father avoided Uncle Kolya!

Although Uncle Kolya spent some part of each winter in St.

Petersburg, he was restless and he often traveled to France. His frequent trips to Paris and the photograph I saw on his desk suggest a French mistress.

In St. Petersburg Uncle Kolya's reputation for acerbic wit made him a familiar figure at the English Club and the Café de Paris. Among those who found his conversation rewarding was Maurice Paléologue, the last French ambassador to the Russian Court. In his book, *An Ambassador's Memoirs*, he gives his impressions of my uncle. Particularly striking, he writes, was Uncle Kolya's "paradox-loving imagination [which] he occasionally reveals with the spontaneity and genius of a Rivarol." Paléologue was referring to the 18th century epigrammatist unrivaled in France for his sharp comment.

One day when the ambassador was giving Uncle Kolya a lift home in his car, they drove past Falconet's famous statue of Peter the Great. To his surprise, my uncle called Peter I " 'the greatest revolutionary of modern times' "—not a true reformer. Why? Because Peter, he explained, attacked national traditions and customs, was intent on destroying the past. " 'A true reformer'," Paléologue quotes him as saying, " 'allows for the past. . .is cautious in his changes and paves the way for the future. . .' "

As might be expected, Uncle Kolya was not circumspect. Friends cautioned him: his barbed remarks, they warned, might lead to trouble, even involve him in a duel. He did not curb his tongue; instead, heeding their counsel, he practiced daily with rapier and pistol. These skills were of no avail to him against the violence of a revolutionary mob. His death in 1918 came only a few days after he missed a special train on which he was to leave Petrograd and Communist territory.

Uncle Fedya—Feodor Nikolayevich Bezak—was Mother's youngest brother. He was better adjusted than the other two. An officer in the Chevalier Garde, he married a daughter of the regiment. In 1902, he retired, a colonel, to take care of family affairs. He then moved to his estate near Kiev and became marshal of nobility in the area. Shortly afterwards, he was elected to the Duma. When the Revolution broke out, he took his family to Nice where his practical bent helped him to make his way as a certified public accountant.

I see in the lives of Uncle Sasha and Uncle Kolya a great waste of talent. Accomplished and well educated as they were, they failed to find a way to bring their abilities to any real service to society. No doubt there were many others like them in Russia at the time.

When Uncle Sasha and Uncle Kolya came to see us, they frequently fussed over Mother. They brought her chocolates, inquired about her health, and complimented her on this and that, especially on her looks. However, they seldom addressed serious conversation to her; they treated her like a child. It would seem that when they were growing up, they babied and teased her, maintaining that she had no mind of her own. This attitude of belittling women's intelligence was not unusual in that era.

In self-defense, Mother parried every question, no matter how inaccurate her answer. My uncles were amused. When Mother married, she found such an approach to problems did not work so well in running a household. With typical Bozak tenacity, however, she persevered. At times she seemed to have a faculty for doing the wrong thing. An incident that occurred when I was twelve is typical.

It was summer and my tutor was reading aloud to me in my room. Mother happened to walk past. She stopped to ask what he was reading.

"Chekhov's *The Darling*," he answered.

She put her foot down: "Absolutely not!" Probably Mother thought the stories of the earthy doctor were too risqué. She then tried to persuade Nils to remove the *Complete Works of Chekhov* from his shelves. He reacted as if he hadn't heard. As it turned out, Mother's attitude increased my interest in Chekhov.

Such incidents were frequent. When we appealed to Father to right some wrong, he invariably sided with Mother. He did not want to get involved as he was home so seldom. Such an attitude left us feeling trapped.

Nils's reaction was to withdraw. Mine was a healthier one: I rebelled. Before I was five, I had tantrums. After that, from time to time, I became unruly. Mother called it wild. Then Mother reminded me that before I was born she had so wished for a girl. It hurt deeply every time she said she would have preferred a girl to me. I must have violently repressed my feelings of resentment and dismay.

Later on, the anger came out in various ways when an occasion presented itself. Once, in the German resort of Bad Homburg, when I was seven, I was disappointed to be left out of a party. I ran away and hid in a wing of the hotel, and stayed there until late at night. Surely, I hoped, Mother was suffering as she had made me suffer. Surely she would welcome me back with open arms. Not at all: I got a scolding and no dessert.

Again in Geneva, when I thought we were going on an excursion to Mont Blanc and found it was only Mont Salève, I was indignant. Nobody had bothered to explain to me that Mont Blanc didn't lend itself to family expeditions. In protest, I stood on one foot in the *finiculaire* all the way to the top of Mont Salève, a special kind of masochism. In vain did Mother urge me to sit down.

Resistance to Mother became more intense as time went on. Still, Mother held to her own way of doing things. During the quarrels that ensued, we usually did not speak to each other for several days—a disgruntled child and a nettled mother. After a time Mother would say she couldn't stand people with long faces and proposed that we kiss and make up. And we did.

Now that I have worked through some of my problems in life, I can feel a degree of sympathy for Mother and realize that she had a number of very serious problems beyond those brought on by Father's prolonged absences. Perhaps my oldest brother's mental condition was just one problem too many. Georges was four years older than Nils and eight years older than I. Though physically fit, he failed to develop mentally. Mother and Father had taken him from doctor to doctor all over Europe. Nils and I went along. Georges had many operations, but nothing seemed to help. His mental level remained that of a not-too-bright five-year-old.

Perhaps this is the point to mention that Georges had a most unusual mathematical skill. I believe that today such a person might be called an idiot savant. The family discovered Georges' strange capacity when he asked for calendars for Christmas. It turned out that, when given any date in any year, he could correctly name the day of the week on which it fell. He gave the answer without even a moment's hesitation.

As it became apparent that medicine could not help Georges, Mother sought out Christian Science and became one of the first Christian Scientists in Russia. Perhaps her new faith helped her to take what must have been a difficult step. I was still small when she decided that it would be better if Georges lived with an attendant apart from the family. My Grandmother Bezak offered to have him live in her apartment nearby. That is where Georges stayed most of the time.

So Nils and I seldom saw Georges except in the summer. When I think of doe-eyed, gangly Georges with his sweet, vapid smile, I still feel a twinge of remorse for something that happened sixty years ago. I was fourteen and Georges, twenty-two. Proud of my newly acquired knowledge of wrestling, I offered to take on Georges. He willingly joined in with the simple goodwill of a puppy at play. In no time at all, my new wrestling hold had tossed Georges to the ground. For my punishment, I can still see his hurt, bewildered expression.

Mother had another serious problem that Christian Science apparently helped her to bear. Though she and Father were careful to keep up appearances, they were both frustrated in their relations as man and wife. I knew nothing of this as a child, but one day when I was in my early teens, Mother surprised me by telling me that she had once considered divorcing Father. She probably had not intended to confide in me. Possibly, under some emotional stress the information slipped out. She also said that her close friend, Nini Voyeikov, had talked her out of it. I surmise that there was another woman—perhaps several—for Father was quite dashing and appreciated a pretty face and an attractive figure. What Mother said led me to conclude that my parents did not sleep together any more. At the time I was too young to grasp the implications, but there were many signs I registered unconsciously. For one thing, Father's dressing room contained a single bed on which he said he rested after lunch. Yet, when he was home on leave, I always found him in his dressing room before breakfast in the morning.

No doubt Mother felt neglected by Father's long absences. Her feeling of hurt could only have been compounded by the knowledge that she had been a court beauty. As lady-in-waiting to Empress Maria Feodorovna, with her petite figure in traditional court dress, she would surely have drawn many an admiring glance. No one ever knew, I suspect, how neglected Mother really felt.

I now see that Mother's seeming helplessness in response to her brothers' teasing gave no indication of her true character. Nor did her hit-or-miss arbitrariness in handling us.

Perhaps all along her tenacity was the real key to her nature.

When the Revolution struck, she showed how well she could stand up to adversity and proved that she was not helpless in the least. From having everything done for her—she had not even brushed her own hair until we left Russia—she adjusted to a whole new way of life. Not only did she learn to cook and keep house, but she taught English to French people and French to English people, and so learned to carry her own load in the world. And she never complained, not even once. Best of all, she had Father back again.

6

VASILIEVSKOYE,
OUR COUNTRY HOME

Father was one of the early camera enthusiasts in Russia. I
have a picture of him as a young officer with his old-
fashioned box camera. Later he had a Kodak. Sometimes,
using a special attachment, he included himself in the picture.
That is the way he got the snapshots of himself with the Tsar
and his daughters in a haystack near Mogilev a few months
before the Revolution. His equipment was simple, and his access to the Tsar made for interesting subjects.

Vasilievskoye was another subject for his camera. Father
had a special feeling for the estate. Not only was it beautiful;
it was his ancestral home. The very fact that, in buying it
from his uncle, he had contravened fate was a source of satisfaction to him. He knew his grandmother had intended it for
him and not for her unmarried son.

The estate was near Smolensk, about two hundred miles
west of Moscow. When we went there in June, we took the
night train from the Capital. By noon of the following day, we

arrived at the Tiomkino railroad station. The train made a special stop to let us off. The rest of our journey to Vasilievskoye, a distance of about twelve miles, would be made by carriage.

On the station platform to welcome us was Makar Savelich, the chubby, jovial stationmaster who was also the postmaster for the area. He greeted us effusively, kissed Mother's hand, and ceremoniously escorted us outside the station. There, waiting for us were three troikas. The first, drawn by three white horses, was presided over by Foma, dressed for the occasion in a black tunic over a white shirt with a red feather in his cap. He was proud to have been chosen head coachman and was meticulous in keeping carriages and horses in tip-top shape. Mother usually traveled in this carriage with Nils. I followed in a second carriage, accompanied by a governess or tutor. The other members of the party, such as Mother's maid, came in the third. There was also a cart for the luggage. Danila and Yegor would go ahead the day before to make everything ready for our arrival.

We all were tired but excited on this last lap of the journey. Only twelve miles to reach Vasilievskoye. But what twelve miles! Bumping along on an incredibly rutted and uneven dirt road. It took two hours to go from Tiomkino to the estate. At first the road stretched through what seemed endless fields of rye, then woods, and across more fields. We passed through two villages seemingly deserted but for children and a few older people; everyone else was off working in the fields. The children, ragged, stood in the doorways of their *izbas*, log cabins with thatched roofs, and followed our progress with curious, sullen stares.

Once, after the rain, the mud in one of the villages was so deep that the horses had to strain to get the carriages through. The first time our French governess, Mlle. Labouré, came with us, she felt affronted. She thought that taking her along these roads was some sort of mean trick. Perhaps this was the way Russians expressed their sense of humor. She could not quite believe roads could be that bad.

When we had passed the second village, we were near home. Once through the gates of the estate, the carriages circled a pond in front of the house. And then, with Foma setting the pace, all three carriages rolled forward at top speed. Foma liked to pull up in front of the veranda with a flourish.

Mlle. Labouré was incredulous that first time she came to Vasilievskoye. For here, in remote, provincial Russia, ostensibly in the middle of nowhere, was a handsome, two-story mansion set off by carefully landscaped grounds.

"Mais ça," she exclaimed, *"c'est un château!"*

Her exclamation of surprise was natural. Vasilievskoye could easily have been taken for the home of some *grand seigneur* elsewhere in Europe. And yet Vasilievskoye harmonized with its surroundings.

There was a certain elegance about the house, a lightness and a warmth of color in its sandstone exterior. The classical simplicity of its design was characteristic of the Palladian style favored by Charles Cameron, a Scottish architect popular in Russia at the time Vasilievskoye was built. On each side of the main house was a guest house. Behind the one to the left was a separate structure housing the kitchen and servants' quarters. A wooden platform connected the kitchen with the main house.

Beyond the guest house on the right were the stables, shielded by shrubbery and trees. Here were kept a dozen or more horses, Nils's pony, and my donkey. Nearby were the greenhouses and the lodgings of the head gardener, Vinogradov. Then came the vegetable garden, and still farther off, the home of our steward, Semyonov. The dairy farm lay beyond that.

Vasilievskoye was named for the man who built it, Count

Vasili Vasilievich Orlov-Denisov, Father's great-grandfather. He is my most illustrious ancestor, and I like to think that he influenced my life. Born on the Don, son of a Don Cossack general, he himself became a general at thirty-one. The times seem to have brought out his abilities.

Father was pleased and proud to have so colorful an ancestor and often talked to Nils and me about him. Two of his exploits stick in my mind. One of them occurred in 1809 during Russia's war with Sweden. In one of the last decisive battles of that war, Orlov-Denisov led two regiments of Cossack horsemen across the frozen Gulf of Finland at night in a snowstorm. The action took the Swedish army by surprise. His service record soon noted that he operated best on his own. "Count Orlov-Denisov should not be hampered too much by directives from above," it stated.

When Napoleon moved on Russia, Orlov-Denisov, who meanwhile had retired and built Vasilievskoye, was recalled to duty. He engaged the French troops as they passed through the area on their way to Moscow. Two small cannon that flanked the manor house served as a reminder of that time; Orlov-Denisov had captured them from the French army. As a small boy I sometimes sat on one of them. He also captured Marshal Murat's field kitchen. It was kept in our barn for many years before Father gave it to a museum in Moscow.

The second outstanding incident in Orlov-Denisov's career came when Napoleon's army had captured Moscow. In an early morning surprise attack, he and his Cossack cavalry galloped upon a French camp at Tarutino near Moscow and routed it. By this action, says Tolstoy in *War and Peace,* Orlov-Denisov turned the tide and touched off the retreat of the French from Russia. Subsequently, he was officially designated a Hero of the Napoleonic War.

"A remarkable man!" Father would exclaim. "A legendary figure!" He marvelled at Orlov-Denisov's daring, spoke of his dash, resourcefulness, and courage. What I most admired was his independence of spirit. As Tolstoy pictured him, Vasili Vasilievich was not impressed by rank or power. I wanted to be like that. To fend off Mother's arbitrary ways, I early discovered the need to make up my own mind. This ancestor bolstered me.

Orlov-Denisov had spared neither expense nor effort when he built his country home. The manor house had large, airy rooms with high ceilings. In keeping with the period, the ceilings were decorated with classic designs in pastel colors. The house was lighted at night by Alladin lamps. They were surprisingly bright, even brighter than our electric lights in the city. In the attic was a large reservoir for storing water, pumped up manually from below. By force of gravity, it went down from the reservoir through pipes to serve the two bathrooms and the pantry. Rainwater from the roof was also collected in the reservoir. Drinking water came from a spring. Even so, it had to be filtered and sometimes boiled. One had to be careful as there was a constant threat of cholera and typhoid. Everybody was aware that Tchaikovsky had died of cholera from drinking tap water.

During the first nine years of my life I spent every summer at Vasilievskoye. An early picture Father took of me shows a pudgy baby propped up in his carriage. He looks intently at the camera. Beside the carriage stands a hearty, young woman in an embroidered peasant dress—the nurse by whom I was breast-fed. An older, earthier-looking woman in a crisp, white uniform, the regular nurse, stands on the other side of the carriage, looking proprietary. In the background is a large veranda, shaded by an awning, the entrance to the manor house at Vasilievskoye. On the veranda, with arms akimbo, stands Mother. She smiles as she contemplates the group below. One cannot tell by looking at the picture that she is the baby's mother, so apart is she from the scene.

One of my earliest memories is of Vasilievskoye at night. I

am in bed, but still awake. The room is dark, and I am apprehensive. The silence is oppressive. Suddenly, out of the darkness, comes the mournful sound of Vasilievskoye's church bell. One lonely stroke and then a pause, and then I hear the bell again, and yet again. It must be ten o'clock. I'm not quite sure. I have already ducked under the covers. I hold my breath and listen. The church, I know, is half a mile away. Around it is a cemetery, and I'm afraid of cemeteries. The bell sounds melancholy, and who can tell what ghosts or other furtive creatures may be around. I've heard about them from Mother's maid. She says the souls of the departed linger about for forty days. Her stories scare me. And now the bell has stopped. Cautiously I bring my head out from under the covers, stare into the darkness, and listen. All I hear is a familiar, reassuring sound: the clamor of Vasilievskoye's frogs out in the pond.

In another vision from the past, I see myself with rod and line on my way to the river just beyond the meadow. I spent many happy hours there on the riverbank, perched high up in a tree that overhung the water. I cast my line. I have a bite. The excitement of the moment runs through me like an electric shock. I jerk the rod. Sometimes I catch the fish; sometimes it gets away. It doesn't really matter. The air is warm. There is a rustling of leaves around me, faint and soothing. I am happy just to sit there in the tree.

I liked to be alone and often sought out secret hiding places. One of these was in a deep ravine between the house and the river. A narrow bridge of white birch led across the ravine to a gazebo overlooking the river. Down below, the ravine was thick with bushes and poison vines. I managed to hack my way through this underbrush to a secret hiding place where no one could find me. There I made a little house of my own. I felt safe. I knew Mother was allergic to the poison weed.

I spent much time wandering about during our summers in

Vasilievskoye. One morning after breakfast I was walking along in the sunshine. I carried a small rifle Father had given me. I was eight, and it was my first rifle. As I came down the path, I saw a sparrow perched on a tree. I took aim and fired. For a few moments I thought I had missed. Then I noticed the blood dripping from the branch. The sight of it overwhelmed me. The sparrow had been a living thing. I had not really meant to kill it; nor even to hurt it. I was only trying out my new rifle.

Some days I explored the park's shady paths and allées, curious to know where they led. One time I walked as far as I could go and came to a fence on the edge of our estate. Beyond stretched a field. Far away, on the horizon, was a house. There lived our closest neighbors, the Petrovs. They had two children my own age, Masha and Petya. Once we called on them with Mother, and they returned the call. There was no further contact. When I asked Mother to arrange for me to play with the Petrov children, she put me off. Later I learned the Petrovs were rural gentry and of a different social milieu from us. "They are provincials," Mother said, "and there is nothing really to talk to them about." There the matter ended, though I continued to go to the edge of the park to gaze across the field toward that distant house.

Vasilievskoye's strawberry patch brings back memories. When I was six I learned to ride a bicycle, and every morning I raced our black fox terrier, Koubik, past the greenhouses to the vegetable garden. He, too, had a great liking for strawberries and was adept at picking off the ripe ones. I tried to get there first. He didn't mind. We both enjoyed the chase. We understood each other.

On the way back I sometimes stopped to chat with the head coachman. Foma was a big, burly man with red hair and searching eyes. He knew about many things—not only about horses, but about fishing and the weather. It was he who told me that for use in a troika horses had to be specially picked and trained to pull together. When horses are harnessed three abreast, he explained, the center horse, which is the largest of the three, must be taught to trot when the outer horses gallop, and walk when they trot. I was surprised to learn that the two outer horses are trained to pull sideways.

On my way back from the stables I sometimes made a detour past the greenhouses. Though Mother had forbidden me to go inside, whenever I found a window open I managed to squeeze myself through. Mother had had the greenhouses locked when she discovered that I helped myself to the hothouse grapes and to the peaches. Father had ordered that even she was to take none of Vasilievskoye's produce without reporting her "purchase" to the steward. Such a requirement Mother considered absurd even if Father said it was necessary for accounting purposes. However that may be, her prohibition made filching the fruit even more tempting than before.

In midsummer, on my seventh name-day—the birthday of Saint Paul—the steward, Semyonov, made me a present of a baby pig. I was delighted. I kept it in an enclosure behind the kitchen. I called my pet Svinyusha, an endearing term for "little pig." I gave it apples, talked to it. It grunted back as if to show it liked my company.

The summer was already ending. We were about to leave. A week or so before our departure, we were served roast pig. I was disgusted. Maybe a brother or a sister of Svinyusha, I thought, and wouldn't touch the dish. After the meal a sudden foreboding made me run to the enclosure. It was empty. Svinyusha was gone. In anguish I stormed into the kitchen. Danila was apologetic. When I pressed him he admitted that the roast pig we had been served was my own Svinyusha. Mother had ordered it. "After all," he quoted her as saying, "we can't take a pig back with us to our apartment." I was stunned, and I vanished into the park. I hid in the ravine, consoling myself with the thought that no one could find me there. When I came home I had chewed off part of my fingernails.

The solace I found in the Russian countryside helped me. Much of the time at Vasilievskoye I was left to myself. Nobody minded if I wandered off. I might just find some mushrooms for Danila's mushroom pie. Nobody came running after me.

As I think back to these summers in the country, I realize there was a special quality about Vasilievskoye—a quality I absorbed from everything around me: from the birch trees and fragrant linden; from the country people who worked on the estate; from my nurse, Pasha.

Vasilievskoye seemed made for entertaining. And, as Father told us, when Vasili Vasilievich brought his beautiful bride there, the glamorous Countess Vasilieva, the estate was the scene of many gay parties. Now there was no social life at all, and few visitors.

An infrequent caller was Father Arkadi. He was the priest at the Russian Orthodox church outside Vasilievskoye's gate, built by Orlov-Denisov for the people on the estate and in the neighboring villages. Ever since his time the family had contributed to its support. I remember Father Arkadi as rosy-cheeked and awkward. He was self-conscious, too, and when he drank tea he sipped it noisily from the saucer. Unfortunately, he was dull. Mother felt that, if she had to invite him, one visit each summer was enough.

Another caller was our postmaster–stationmaster, Makar Savelich. Now and then he took advantage of his postmaster's telephone to invite himself to tea on the pretext of delivering the mail in person. Mother found Makar Savelich's pushy joviality offensive, but she couldn't resist his visits. He always came primed with gossip. And no wonder! He steamed open all our mail and, although he never acknowledged actually reading our correspondence, his oblique references showed that he had.

"Times are certainly uncertain," he would declare. "And I do hope the plans of your esteemed brother, Nikolai Nikolayevich, work out to his complete advantage and, I might say, his satisfaction." Just a few days before, Uncle Kolya had written that he was tired of the bureaucrats he had to deal with and was quitting the Ministry of the Interior.

Or else, on the level of local gossip, he would say: "Your maid, Katyusha, has certainly found herself a fine, young man! What! She has not yet told you she is to be married? Well, I declare! Well, well! You must not let her know I told you. I beg you."

Although indignant, Mother could not resist listening to him, and when she asked Father to reprimand the man, she did so only half-heartedly. She wasn't sure she wanted this avenue of information cut off altogether. Father, in turn, was not inclined to reprimand Makar Savelich for reading our mail since his own mail didn't pass through the postmaster's hands. It went to Cannes, where he was stationed during these years. Besides, he had a certain fondness for Makar Savelich. Father liked to tell how he became godfather to the postmaster's son. This is the story as he told it.

Once, during winter, Father had traveled to Vasilievskoye to look over some repairs. On his way back he was delayed by a snowstorm. The train was late, and he was stranded for several hours in the railroad station at Tiomkino. Makar Savelich was, as usual, in an expansive mood. Over a glass of tea he confided to Father his ardent desire for a child.

"I hope your wish is granted," said Father sympathetically as he warmed himself in front of the potbellied stove.

"Alas, God has apparently not so decreed," said the postmaster, and then his eyes fell on a copy of *La Vie Parisienne*

Father had finished reading. "May I?" he asked. He picked up the magazine and leafed through its pages. The issue included pictures of glamorous showgirls suggestively disrobed. "Ah-h-h!" he sighed. "What a collection! We have nothing like that in Russia!"

Amused, Father offered him the magazine. "You may have it," he said. "I'm through with it." Just then the train came in, and Father left.

The following winter Father again had to make a hurried trip to Vasilievskoye. The stationmaster greeted him effusively. "I cannot tell you how indebted I am to you, Your Excellency," he said beaming.

"Indebted?"

"The magazine you left me with those pictures . . ."

"Well?"

"With your help, God has been kind to us. Yes, just three months ago my wife presented me with a fine son . . ."

"Congratulations."

". . . and I beg of you, Your Excellency, since in a manner of speaking you had a part in it, please do us the honor, the great honor, to be the child's godfather."

In his belief in God's goodness, Makar Savelich was not too different from the peasants. As they saw it, God took a hand in their lives. If you lived a good life, God was benign. And if you didn't and God was angry, there might be some way to placate Him.

We saw the peasants every day, but seldom exchanged words. We'd pass them in the fields when we went fishing. And sometimes our fire engine was called in to cope with a village fire. The fires usually occurred at night. Then the men pumped furiously, but with little result. We stood watching the blaze consume first the thatched roofs, then the walls of the log cabins. Strangely, the owners seemed resigned to their fate: "It is God's will," they would say. In much the same manner Nicholas II would approach his abdication.

When I was old enough to mount the pony and join the others on horseback, we sometimes came upon peasants plowing the fields; or, again, a few miles downstream, watering their horses. Once in a while a group of men from a neighboring village came to see Father with a petition or grievance. Their words were respectful; their tone, surly. They might want to borrow some agricultural implement, or they might be asking permission for their cows to cross a meadow. Their business was usually minor, but Father was always on the defensive with them.

Peasant women were around more often than the men. Many of them were hired by the day to work in the gardens. I used to see them raking up the grass clippings. They were colorful in their peasant dresses and bright head scarves as they moved along in unison with their wooden rakes. They often sang as they worked. Some threw bantering remarks at Nils and me, which we tried to return in kind. Mother did not know how to talk to them in a natural way, so when she happened to be present everybody was ill at ease.

Most of the congregation of Vasilievskoye's church came from the village of Godnevo across the river. There every Sunday we saw peasants at mass. Otherwise, we had very little contact with them. I knew no peasant children in all the summers we spent at Vasilievskoye.

The only child of my own age with whom I played was Vanya Semyonov, the steward's son. He once approached me shyly when I was fishing, climbed up on a branch near me, produced a line, and cast it next to mine. Neither of us spoke at first. Then Vanya said, "The fish aren't biting very well today, are they? Maybe there'll be a thunderstorm." His remark broke the ice.

Following this incident we went around together a good

deal. But just as his family was socially and intellectually miles removed from the outlook and interests of the peasants, so also was my family's style of life, concerns, and point of view almost on a different plane of being from that of the steward and his family. Somehow there always was a distance, a constraint between Vanya and me, and the relationship never deepened.

I came to understand the nature of the gap between us some time later, when I was back in Saint Petersburg and had received a letter from Vanya. He wrote: "Your Excellency, I take the liberty of writing you to beg you to grant me a request. . . ." The letter went on to state that he was applying to a technical school and that my recommendation would help him to get admitted.

It was a shock and a disappointment to be addressed as "Your Excellency" by someone with whom I had climbed trees, gone fishing, and hunted for mushrooms. For the first time I realized that I was cut off from some people through no will of my own. Even in the world of children, it seems, there were inferiors, equals, and superiors.

As a practical matter I could do nothing to help Vanya without enlisting the cooperation of my parents. That was hard to do. They couldn't have been more indifferent. "His father dictated the letter," Mother said contemptuously, "and it should never have been addressed to you in the first place." The matter ended there. There was nothing I could say, so I didn't answer the letter. Actually, answering letters is something I never did.

At Vasilievskoye I also played with Nils. Although his seemingly unemotional approach was alien to my more spontaneous nature, we spent a lot of time together. We bicycled around together, went rowing on the river, played croquet. He usually beat me at croquet, as he did at cards and practi-

Manor house on our country estate, Vasilievskoye, near Smolensk, built in 1810, about 200 miles west of Moscow. (1902)

Troika at entrance to the estate, with Foma the head coachman. (1902)

These pictures were taken by my father.

Vasilievskoye interior. (1904)

The Grabbe family: Father, George, Nils
standing, Mother, author on right. (1904)

The author, aged six months, with nurses. The wet nurse is wearing traditional Russian costume. The author's mother is on the verandah in the background. (1902)

Local peasant women hired to do the haying. (1907)

Retired coachman on the estate. (1907)

The author's grandmother, Maria Feodorovna Bezak, née Louginina. (1908)

Deacon, priest and sexton. (1908)

The author with his father. (1909)

The author and brother, Nils. (1910)

Uncle Sasha—Alexander Nikolayevich Bezak, Mother's oldest brother. (1910)

Uncle Kolya—Nicolai Nikolayevich Bezak, Mother's youngest brother with author and Nils in ballroom of St. Petersburg apartment. (1905)

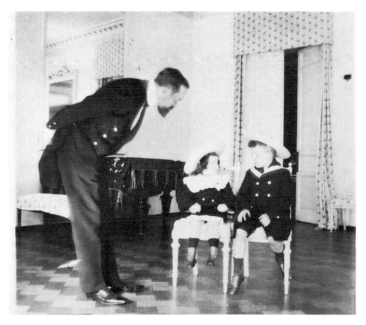

Peasant women after church service. Village simpleton is in foreground, right. (1908)

cally everything else, making me feel inadequate. But then I did not allow for the fact that he was older.

What we had most in common was music. Even in his early teens he played the piano well. He could pick up almost anything by ear and could read music with ease. I had none of these skills and did not believe I could ever acquire them. During the winter months we both took piano lessons. Nils practiced diligently. When I heard the teacher coming, I hid under the grand piano. Eventually, Mother got tired of insisting and let me give up piano lessons altogether. I came out of these lessons at least able to play a few simple pieces. I learned later on to pick up some by ear—a skill that served me well.

It wasn't only in music that I felt inferior to Nils, but scholastically and socially as well. Nils was good-looking with a fine figure, brown eyes, and black curly hair. For my age, I had ears that rather protruded and hair so red that once a boy skating past me yelled: "There's a house on fire!" Nils danced well, though he did not like to dance. I longed to be more graceful at those Sunday dancing classes back in St. Petersburg. Nils was good in school, too. He knew five languages, including Latin. I couldn't spell too well—even in Russian. He excelled in mathematics, I didn't. He had a fine memory and kept himself informed on current events. He not only read the newspapers of the Right, but of the Left as well, to our parents' sardonic amusement. How could they cope with the likes of Nils? After the Revolution they could not even shield his sensitive nature from emigré pressure to join the White Army.

To outward appearances, everything came easily to Nils. How could I struggle against such superiority? Finding no answer, I felt defeated and was aware that an undercurrent of hostility ran through our relationship. My anger was repressed, but it came to the surface when Mother boasted about Nils. I was convinced that she preferred him to me; and when she showed him off, I felt rage, an all-consuming help-less rage. In my frustration and jealousy I once got the parlor maid down on the floor, trying to overpower her, but she shook herself free. "Hey," she said, turning toward me as she paused prettily in the doorway, "You're quite strong for your age . . ." She smiled approvingly. "But still a little bit too young, you know." I was perhaps ten at the time. Her remark somehow comforted me.

Our activities at Vasilievskoye seldom included Georges, our older brother. Perhaps we did not know just how to han-dle him or what to say to him. Georges lived on the first floor with his companion-tutor, Surem Gerasimovich Chilingarov, a native of the Caucasus who claimed a special interest in Georges' case because he had once studied medicine. How he and Georges spent their time I don't remember, if I ever knew, except that both always came in for dinner with the family in the downstairs dining room.

Georges, at nineteen, was handsome and physically nor-mal, but his conversation was very limited. In our eyes he was just one of those facts of life that had to be accepted, not questioned. Explaining his condition, Mother told us once that when he was a baby his nurse dropped him on his head. We never questioned her story or wanted to know more.

At Vasilievskoye it sometimes rained for days and maybe weeks on end. When the rain stopped, there was a rush to get outdoors. The reappearance of the sun called for a celebra-tion. We usually went on a picnic. Some old peasant always knew, or thought he knew, the exact spot where a treasure had once been buried. So we started out to the designated spot, adults and children, some in carriages and some on horseback. We ate our picnic lunch seated around a tablecloth spread on the grass, then dug into the ground, pretending we might come upon a cache of silver coin. Toward evening we would go home, pleasantly exhausted even if we had found nothing.

On one such expedition, an accident occurred. One of the horses kicked our terrier Koubik. He died before we could get him home. Driving back we were subdued. Hardly anyone spoke.

At noon the next day, a solemn procession started from the house. First came the footman, Dourakov, carrying a box with Koubik's remains. Then came Mother with Georges and Nils and me, and Mother's Christian Science friends who were visiting us, and then Monsieur Honorat, our French tutor, and Chilingarov. At a respectful distance behind the family walked the servants, the gardeners, the coachman, and even some peasant women attracted by the unusual event. Solemnly the procession crossed the little birch bridge to one of the pond's wooded islands, where the gravesite for Koubik had already been prepared. Monsieur Honorat delivered a short eulogy in French, trying with no great success to share in our grief. Then Koubik was buried. It was a sad day.

That afternoon I came upon Monsieur Honorat sitting on a garden bench. He seemed to be examining something. As I came closer, I realized what he was doing. He had caught a large fly and, slowly, methodically, was tearing off one wing, and then another, and then the creature's legs. As the fly was still alive, I was revolted and hurried past with the pretence that I had seen nothing. Previously, I had neither liked nor disliked the French tutor. After this incident, I avoided him. I couldn't stand him anymore.

Why are so many tutors sadistic? Certainly this uprooted Frenchman was! Did being far from his homeland have anything to do with it? I was lucky Mr. Honorat took out his frustrations on a fly rather than on me. Far worse would be the Irishman, Mr. Boyle, soon to come into my life. Fortunately for me, my Russian tutors would be kindly and understanding. Now I can look back and see that when Koukoulya and, later, Vladimir Aleksan'ch came into our household each in his way would command my respect and help me to grow. Mr. Honorat had the opposite effect—and so would the hated Mr. Boyle.

I didn't have to avoid Mr. Honorat for long. Summer was nearly over at the time of Kubik's funeral.

Several days later Father told us that this summer would be our last at Vasilievskoye. Over the years he had been gradually disposing of the arable land, selling it to the peasants on the installment plan, and he had just sold what was left of the estate, together with the manor house and grounds, to a rich Moscow merchant. From then on, he said, we would be spending our summers at Bogorodskoye, Mother's small estate southeast of Moscow. His announcement was a blow to all of us. Vasilievskoye was our second home. It was too costly to keep up, Father said. He needed the money for his remodeling enterprises in the city.

And so came the time to say good-bye. It was a bright September day. Our luggage had been piled near the front entrance. Nils and I ran through all the rooms to say farewell to them. When we were ready to leave, we sat down, according to Russian custom, as a family group, for a moment of prayer. *"Noo, s'Bogom,"* said Father, getting up and crossing himself—"God go with us." Silently we piled into the waiting troikas. The staff of the estate, standing in front of the veranda, took off their hats. Nils shouted, "Good-bye, good-bye!" Foma flicked his whip, and we were off; the little bells on the horses' harness jingled softly.

Autumn came early that year. The beech trees were already shedding their leaves. At the end of the first mile we neared the ravine. There the vines had turned crimson. As we drove on, I caught a last glimpse of the manor house. I did not know at the time that I was saying good-bye to a style of life—not just to Vasilievskoye.

The manor house would soon burn to the ground. Father heard that the Moscow merchant, as if to chide him for selling his ancestral home, had set it on fire to collect insurance. The Revolution finished off the rest. The trees in the park were chopped down, the greenhouses smashed, and before long there was nothing left. Nothing that is, but a memory. That would remain.

7

MY TUTOR, KOUKOULYA

"Fresh air is good for you," Mother used to say as she marched me off every morning with governess or tutor. I objected to these outdoor walks just as I balked at taking a spoonful of cod-liver oil before lunch. But once Koukoulya became my tutor, I stopped resisting cod-liver oil and the daily walks.

I was very fond of Mikhail Dimitrievich Kryzhanovsky. I loved the stories he told me during our walks. After a time I thought up a special name for him, an affectionate diminutive: Koukoulya.

He had been recommended to Father by the wife of a fellow officer. I later heard a rumor that Koukoulya had had an affair with her. I doubt if Mother knew about that. She saw him as a man of middle height who had a pleasing manner and a black mustache. What mattered to her was that he came with a good reference. His equivocal status in the household— neither servant nor equal—did not concern her She would never learn to know him better.

Koukoulya was a kindly, unassuming man, and very easygoing. He blurred his *r*'s and was forever running out of cigarettes. I found these qualities endearing. Not so my parents. They were unpleasantly surprised when I flunked my first examination at the *gimnasia* nearby. I was approaching ten, and Mother had arranged a test so she could check up on how much I was learning.

Koukoulya, it appeared, had failed to teach me to spell correctly or to recite the Ten Commandments in proper order or trace on a map the course of the Gulf Stream. Even after he had assured Father and Mother that everything would be all right (*"Nye bespokoites,"* he had said in true Russian fashion— "Don't worry"), they remained skeptical. Clearly, they had reservations about my tutor, though I had none.

Koukoulya, a native of Nizhni-Novgorod, had a brother who was a tenor at the Imperial Opera, and he, himself, aspired to be an actor. He told me that he hoped some day to play Lopatkin in Chekhov's *Cherry Orchard* and Khlestakhov in Gogol's *Inspector-General*. The enthusiasm with which he spoke about the stage was touched with reverence. His attitude contrasted sharply with that of my parents. They thought of actors and performers as not quite reputable. Such a prejudice was common in Russian society at the time.

In me Koukoulya had a perfect audience for his tales of adventure. In fact, I could hardly wait to get into my outdoor clothes, and no sooner were we outside the house than I would ask him, "What's next? What's going to happen next?"

"Well, let me see," he'd say. "Just where did we leave off?" And he would launch himself upon the next installment of his story.

All of Koukoulya's stories were improvisations. They were so colorful and had so many wonderful elaborations that I never tired of listening to him. The story I remember best, perhaps because it took Koukoulya several months to tell it,

involved a young school teacher who won first prize in a big
lottery. With his prize money he bought a small traveling circus, rented a barge on the Volga, loaded the tent, performers,
and all the animals onto it, and went sailing down the river.
He stopped with his troupe to give performances in all the
towns and hamlets on the way. As part of each performance
he introduced a one-act play, and every time the circus
stopped, some harrowing event occurred: the barge would hit
the pier, toppling the cage that held the bear and letting the
bear escape; the tightrope walker would fall in love with a
local peasant girl and have a deadly fight with the villain to
whom she was betrothed; there would be panic when the tent
caught fire during a performance . . .

Sometimes at the most crucial juncture of the story,
Koukoulya, who usually walked at a brisk pace, would come
to a full stop in front of a motion picture theater. "Would you
like to see this picture?" he would ask, examining the
billboard. "It's about outlaws in the Wild West. . . . Promises
to be interesting. Shall we go in?" He would reach into his
coat pocket, produce some coins, and buy two tickets.

I was more interested in having him continue his story, but
I knew I had to yield. Koukoulya had a weakness for the
movies. He showed a zestful and naive delight in all the hap-
penings presented on the screen, though some of the domes-
tic dramas shown were probably quite trashy. Movies were a
novelty. Already in 1911, neighborhood theaters were spring-
ing up all over the residential areas of St. Petersburg. Some
ran continuous performances. Their programs changed every
week, and I believe we never missed a show. Father and
Mother knew nothing of these expeditions, and I was careful
not to give Koukoulya away.

Sometimes when rain or snow forced us to stay indoors, we
got around to more serious subjects. One of Koukoulya's
duties was to prepare me for military school: I was scheduled

to enter at thirteen. He did his best, and did it in his own way. Instead of teaching me routinely page by page from a textbook, he tried to introduce the subject through some event, some deed, some angle that he judged would capture my imagination. He showed real empathy in this approach.

"About a thousand years ago," Koukoulya once told me, when we were studying early Russian history, "there lived a prince who ruled the Kievan state. His name was Sviatoslav. He was a man of great energy, brave and resourceful, quick as a panther. During his campaigns he slept out of doors, using his saddle as a pillow. He spent much of his time fighting the Khazars. These were nomadic prairie people— Mongols they were—who constantly harassed his state. Eventually he beat them off and broke their power, and I must say, in one respect he was quite different from any other ruler Russia ever had. . . ."

Koukoulya paused significantly. Then he went on: "Sviatoslav abhorred stealth. He never tried to take his enemies by surprise. . . ." Koukoulya paused again. "Instead, what do you suppose he did when he marched against the Khazars?"

"What?" I asked.

"He sent messengers ahead to tell his enemies: 'I come against you!' "

The story made a deep impression. This practice of letting people know when they had trespassed or offended and you were on the move against them appealed to me. I found it admirable, and I made up my mind right then that when I grew up I, too, would wage war that way, out in the open. I told Koukoulya so.

Some time later, during another of our study sessions, I confided that I found the Bible boring. We were reading some passage from the Old Testament and I could hardly keep from fidgeting and yawning. At the time, the Scriptures were taught in every school in Russia. The subject was called *Zakon*

Bozhyi, the Law of God. My illustrated textbook had on its first page a colored drawing of a benign old gentleman in flowing robes with his arms outstretched. He seemed to float on a pellucid cloud—no doubt the artist's concept of God in the act of Creation.

"Perhaps you are not acquainted with passages that aren't boring," said Koukoulya. "Some sentiments here, for instance . . ." He picked up a copy of the New Testament and fingered through its pages, "are quite beautiful . . . quite worthy of your attention." He read: " 'Blessed are the humble, for they shall inherit the earth. . . .' " He went on reading.

Blessed are the humble! I immediately liked the idea. It put the powerful, the arrogant, the haughty in their proper place. It was a warning against self-importance and a reminder of how very frail and vulnerable man really is.

These thoughts did not occur to me until much later. But even to a little boy, the precept felt right. It was congenial to my temperament and my experience. I liked it.

"You may have heard these teachings of Christ in church," said Koukoulya, "or maybe you did not notice . . ."

"In church?" I murmured trying to recall.

Every Sunday morning during the winter months, Mother took Nils and me to mass. It was held in a private chapel at the home of the Sheremetievs. Several families had a standing invitation to attend. Father never joined us. He seldom went to church except when required by his military duties. Mother apparently saw no inconsistency in being a Christian Scientist and yet going to the Sheremetievs' splendid chapel every Sunday.

I always looked forward to these weekly visits. The Sheremetiev mansion had a fine view of the Neva. I liked to ride their elevator. There was a large ballroom in which I romped, a library two stories high, and many nooks and corners to explore. The chapel was on the third floor. Behind the choir alcove was a spiral stairway of wrought iron; and on the top landing, straddling the railing, sat the bellringer. In his hands he held ropes for half a dozen bells. After the service, he rang the bells in the traditional manner of the Russian Orthodox Church. I liked to watch him and to listen. It was a joyful sound.

Count Aleksander Sheremetiev, our host, was a talented amateur musician. His *a capella* choir was exceptional. He sometimes conducted it himself. Russian church music has a serenity and yet a fullness of emotion that can be very moving. I came to mass willingly in order to hear this music. Besides, I liked to explore the house and enjoyed the delicious communion bread in the form of muffins. There were always some pieces left on a silver tray next to the altar after the service. Unnoticed, I would help myself on my way out.

Nobody had told me what the church service was about; and since I was not especially interested and did not ask, no one took the trouble to explain it to me. Perhaps for this reason, I never, even as an adult, quite understood why praying is associated with going to church and why people feel they have to go to church on Sunday. In our family, curiosity was not encouraged. Children were not enlightened on any subject unless it related to passing school examinations.

I was, however, made to understand when I was still quite small that every night before going to sleep I had to recite my prayers—the Lord's Prayer and a special prayer for the Virgin Mary—or else God would surely strike me down with thunder and lightning. Intimidated by this prospect, I said my prayers dutifully every night. But on my eleventh birthday, I decided it was foolish to mumble prayers mechanically and very fast just to get through with them. Surely, I reasoned, God would not strike me down if I stopped this meaningless ritual. And so one day, gathering up my courage, I went to bed, turned over, and went to sleep.

Next morning I woke up early, jumped out of bed, and ran to Koukoulya's room. He was still asleep. I tugged at his shoulder until he opened his eyes.

"Koukoulya, Koukoulya," I said excitedly, "last night I did not say my prayers. I didn't. And nothing happened. . . ."

"Well," said Koukoulya, yawning and still only half awake. "What did you expect would happen?"

A year later Koukoulya left us to join a theatrical company, and we lost track of him. Then, after the Revolution and our escape abroad, Father got in touch with him again. My parents had had disquieting news about Georges. Emma Fredericks and her father, the elderly Count Fredericks, had taken shelter in our Petrograd apartment after their own home had been sacked. The Fredericks wrote to say that Yegor, our butler, had suddenly departed for Bogorodskoye, Mother's estate, and taken Georges along. They had left in haste, the letter said. We wondered why. All inquiries proved futile. Yegor and Georges had simply disappeared. In desperation, Father wrote to Koukoulya in Petrograd. He told him he had found a way to send money and begged him to locate Georges and bring him out of Russia.

It so happened that my former tutor's theatrical company had closed its doors; Russia was torn by civil war, and he was eager to get out of the country. So he set off at once to look for Georges.

Koukoulya found no trace of Georges at Bogorodskoye, but an old gardener told him that Yegor had left my brother stranded in the manor house. It seems the butler had absconded with the family silver. Further inquiries revealed that Georges had taken shelter in a nearby village.

At that time in Russia, the village simpleton enjoyed a special status, for such a person was regarded in the village as "closer to God" than ordinary mortals. And so it happened that Georges had been able to wander from village to village and was everywhere given food and shelter. Eventually, Koukoulya caught up with him and brought him back to Petrograd.* Father arranged to have both smuggled across the Russian frontier, and they finally reached France.

Father found a sanitarium in the French Alps for Georges to live in; he eventually died there in 1938 of pneumonia. Koukoulya went to live with his brother in Paris. I never saw either of them again, for I had in the meantime emigrated to the United States. But when I heard the good news that Georges had been found, I wrote Koukoulya to add my word of thanks and to say how glad I was to have news of him again.

"Remember," I said in my letter, "the movies we enjoyed together—about outlaws and Indians and the wild goings-on in the American West? Well, dear Koukoulya, believe it or not, here I am in Colorado, right in the middle of the American West. Only I don't 'shoot from the hip' or hold up stagecoaches. I shovel ore in a gold mine near Cripple Creek for four dollars and fifty cents a day."

He answered my letter and said he was very touched that I remembered the name I had used for him when I was small: Koukoulya. How could I ever forget it!

---

*The name of the Russian capital was changed from Saint Petersburg to Petrograd as a result of anti-German feeling brought on by World War I. Saint Petersburg sounded too Germanic, and the name was therefore Russianized. It was changed again to Leningrad in 1924 in honor of the Communist leader.

8

GRANDMOTHER LEAVES US

"Look at this!" Father exclaimed as he set his glass of coffee down on the table. He was holding up the *Peterburgskaya Gazeta* with its bold headline: "TITANIC SINKS. MANY FEARED LOST."

"What a tragedy!" he mused. "Of all things, hitting an iceberg! Who would have thought? . . ."

"Certainly not the captain," said Nils. "Just before sailing, he announced that even God could not sink his ship."

"So he did, so he did," Father concurred. "That's arrogance for you. Tempting Providence! Never wise to do that."

Father took another swallow from his glass, then glanced over at Nils and me. "By the way," he said, lowering his voice. When Father said "by the way" in that tone of voice, Nils and I knew some difficult subject was about to be broached. Father went on. "We're bringing Grandmother here today. . . . A bed will be made up for her in the playroom. She'll be staying a few days . . . until she gets well. She is still very ill, though. It may be pneumonia. Mother thinks we can take better care of her here. So you two had better stay out of the playroom. At least for the present. . . ."

That afternoon our end of the apartment became strangely quiet. The door to the playroom was closed; people went up to it on tiptoe, opened and closed it softly as they went in and out. They spoke in whispers. Doctor Grouss, who had treated Nils and me in the past, came and went. Soon he came again. Around three in the afternoon Mother went into the room, and I did not see her come out again for hours, though I kept a close watch. Emilia, Mother's Estonian maid, brought her some supper on a tray. When Emilia opened the door, I caught a glimpse of Grandmother lying on a bed, shielded from the light by a screen. She was breathing heavily, and her breathing made a strange rasping sound. The door closed before I had a chance to get a better look.

"Grandmother must be very ill," I said to Nils.

"She may die," he commented laconically.

"You think so?"

"Of course," said Nils. "When old people get pneumonia, they usually die." That Grandmother might die had not occurred to me until that moment.

"You really think so?" I asked more urgently.

I did not like hearing Nils say that of course Grandmother might die, as if she were of no concern to him. This was not true, I knew. It was just his manner, which could be exasperating at times—his matter-of-fact way of expressing himself. He always kept his feelings to himself.

He was as fond of Grandmother as I was. Of that I was certain. How could it be otherwise? It would be hard not to like Grandmother. She was so thoughtful, so kind. Always so gentle with Georges. And yet she was firm, but never arbitrary. When there was a quarrel or misunderstanding in the family, she listened to all sides of the argument. In the summer, when we were all together at Vasilievskoye, I used to go to her end of the house when I was puzzled or bothered by something, and she usually straightened it out for me. She seemed to like to be sought out. Not always, of course. Not when she sat at her desk peering through horn-rimmed glasses at some book or article.

Grandmother read a great deal of the time. She knew so much about a lot of things. Books and newspapers and magazines—French, Russian, English, even German—were everywhere—in the bookcase, on the little table near her armchair, even on the floor; and when Grandmother was immersed in her reading, she did not like to be disturbed. At other times she would listen to me, ask questions, talk to me on every imaginable subject. Many were beyond my grasp, such as why she liked certain authors and what it meant to be civilized and how the words we used could affect our behavior—like the English word, *fairness*, for instance. "It is an English concept," she told me, "and it's a good one— *fairness*, I mean. We could use some of it in Russia. But we don't even have a word for it here. . . ."

And now Grandmother was ill. She might even die.

Before supper Uncle Kolya came. He looked preoccupied, and he did not speak to me as he went by. When he left, his eyes were red, and he took out a handkerchief and wiped them hurriedly as if he did not want anyone to notice he was crying.

That evening when I went to bed, I was troubled. Around me in the darkness I imagined all sorts of things—forces unfamiliar and menacing. The night seemed heavy with foreboding, and I tossed a long time before I fell asleep.

The next morning when I got up, the door to the playroom was open and Grandmother was no longer in the room. "Where is Grandmother?" I asked Emilia, who was standing near the window.

"If you go to the ballroom, you'll find her there," said

Emilia. "Your Grandmother, Maria Feodorovna, God rest her soul, died last night." Only instead of saying "died," Emilia used the gentler way Russians have of referring to death. She said, *"Ona skonchalas,"* an expression that derives from the verb *konchat,* to finish, and carries the thought that one has completed one's stay on earth.

Emilia turned on her heels and left the playroom. I stayed there trying to sort out my feelings. Death had never come close to me before. To be sure, Koubik, our dog, had died at Vasilievskoye, and his death had come as a shock to me. But no one I knew, much less anyone close to me, had ever died. I was aware, of course, that people did die. They died when they got old or even not so old, as when they met with an accident or became very ill. Until then I had thought of death as something that happened to other people, not to someone near me. Now death had come close, and I wondered where people went after they died. Where had Grandmother gone? That the hereafter we'd heard about in sacred studies really existed did not seem likely. But where was Grandmother now? At that point I didn't know that no one ever has the answer.

Before sitting down to breakfast, I could not resist looking into the ballroom to see if Grandmother was really there as Emilia had said. Right away I noticed that the grand piano had been pushed to one side. In its place was a raised platform. On the platform was an open coffin and in the coffin lay Grandmother with her eyes closed. A little to one side were several chairs on which sat Mother with Uncle Kolya and Uncle Fedya. They were talking in whispers and at first did not notice me.

I looked at Grandmother. Her face was very white. It was drawn, expressionless, not like her at all. She had always been so animated, so very much alive. I hardly recognized her. As I stood near the coffin, I became aware of the silence in the room, the solemnity of the occasion, the presence of death, there, not five feet away; and suddenly I wanted to leave the room, put distance between me and Grandmother. Seeing her in her coffin brought back oppressive memories of something I had recently read, the story *Viy* by Gogol. A fearsome tale, about a seminarian in the Ukrainian countryside who falls into the clutches of a witch. He frees himself by beating her with a club.

As I stood there, I recalled the sequence of events in the story:

The seminarian, so the tale went, returns to Kiev, still shaky after his experience with the witch. He finds six hefty Cossacks waiting for him there. They have been sent to fetch him on orders of their village chief. The chief's beautiful young daughter has died, the victim of a beating by an unknown assailant. Her dying wish had been to have the seminarian, and no one else, brought to the local church to read prayers over her coffin for three successive nights. On hearing this, the seminarian is frightened and wants to turn back. But by now they have arrived at the Cossack settlement and the dead girl's father won't let him go.

After sunset his fears increase when he is locked inside the church alone with the coffin; and rightly so. Halfway through the first night, the dead girl rises out of the coffin. Grinding her teeth and staring with unseeing eyes, she moves about the church, her arms outstretched as if she were trying to catch someone. Thoroughly scared, the seminarian draws a protective circle around himself, for he has recognized in the dead girl the witch whom he had beaten. Next day he again tries to flee, but he is watched; and so, on the second night, the corpse renews her efforts to get him into her deadly embrace. This time she stands at the very edge of the protective circle, livid with rage and fixing him with her unseeing

greenish eyes. Terrified, the seminarian recites all the exor-
cisms against evil spirits he has ever known, and she at last
retreats to her coffin. On the third night, the witch summons
to her aid all the unearthly creatures of darkness, even the
most awesome monster of them all, the gnome-like Viy. As
morning breaks, the church is found in shambles and the
seminarian, lying prostrate on the stone floor.

Even then, as I stood before Grandmother's coffin, I shud-
dered as I pictured the devastated church, the icons all askew
on the walls, the half-open casket, the seminarian lying sense-
less on the floor, and various batlike creatures caught in their
flight by the coming of day, immobilized grotesquely around
the shattered windowpanes.

Mother's voice broke in on these thoughts. "Come, Pavlik,"
I heard her say. "Come. You may go up and kiss Grandmother's forehead."

Involuntarily, I drew back. I did not want to kiss Grandmother's forehead. But how could I avoid it? Acutely ill at
ease, I dutifully stepped up to the platform and did as Mother
ordered. Grandmother's forehead was cold, and kissing it felt
strange, unpleasant. I tried to tell myself that Grandmother
was not Gogol's witch and that I loved her, but found no
comfort in the thought. Not only was I uneasy; I was physically repelled. I wanted to turn and run.

Mother's voice came to my rescue. "Don't just stand there,"
I heard her say. "Go and have your breakfast."

That day and the next people came to pay their respects.
They looked solemn, offered condolences, and stayed only a
short time. Toward evening Uncle Sasha arrived from abroad.
He sat next to the coffin for a long time, his head bent low,
and said not a word.

Then came the day of the funeral. First there was a short
service at the apartment. It was conducted by an elderly priest

who walked with the help of a cane—an old friend of the family, Mother said. About two dozen people attended this service. When it was over, the coffin was closed by some men in black who appeared as if from nowhere. They carried the coffin down the stairs, and we followed after we had put on our overcoats. The coffin was placed in a hearse drawn by two black horses. The hearse moved forward slowly, and all the mourners followed on foot, first the immediate family, then everybody else. Traffic made way for us, and people in the street crossed themselves as we went by.

The bracing April air felt good, and the faces of the mourners brightened perceptibly as we walked along. Except for the immediate family, whose faces were somber, most people looked jovial, as if taking part in a not-too-unpleasant social occasion. They greeted each other, moved from group to group. Some had come a distance and wanted to take full advantage of the opportunity to exchange the latest family gossip.

After a long walk we came to the Aleksander Nevsky Lavra, a large monastery on the outskirts of the city, three or four miles beyond the Nikolayevsky Railroad Station. Within its grounds was a cemetery. As we passed by the graves, Nils pointed out to me that many people who were well known in the worlds of politics, the theater, and the arts were buried there. "See," he said, drawing my attention to a bas relief of a seagull, "that's the grave of Komissarzhevskaya, famed for her portrayal of Nina in Chekhov's play. A talented actress . . . died early . . . of smallpox."

Before interment, there was a funeral service at the church adjoining the cemetery. A choir of forty monks sang beautifully. The Russian Orthodox funeral service is called *otpevaniye*—singing off. It is long and ends with a most mournful prayer.

Then the coffin was carried from the church, and we all followed it. I kept wondering why I didn't cry during the service. Other people did. Uncle Kolya cried, and so did Mother; probably Nils did, too, though I couldn't be sure. I thought I caught Mother's reproachful look as we left the church.

It had started snowing when we reached the burial place. There was a short service at the grave. Then the coffin was placed in a mausoleum next to my grandfather's crypt. The mausoleum was of red granite, simple and solid looking.

By that time I was very tired and glad to be driven home in Father's new Renault.

9

WHILE FATHER WAS AWAY

Mr. Boyle and I came upon each other soon after Grandmother's death. The meeting was not auspicious.

I had just climbed up to the exercise bar in the doorway of our playroom and was wondering how to get down when I became aware of someone else's presence.

"Why don't you jump?"

The words—in English—startled me. I swung around, piqued by the mocking tone. What was this stranger doing in our home?

He stood there at the entrance to the room, a faint sardonic smile on his thin lips. A man of middle height, blue-eyed, no longer young, he was perhaps in his mid-thirties. He wore a tweed jacket and a brownish tie.

Not knowing who he was, I did not answer. Presently he realized that I had no intention of jumping. So he repeated, this time with a suggestion of finality, as if he expected to be obeyed: "Jump down, why don't you!" He waited a few seconds and, when I made no move, added slowly, "But I can see you are a coward, aren't you?" He turned and left.

I did not know much English at the time, but understood it well enough to get his point. Now angry, I called to Nils, who was in the next room. He helped me from the bar.

"Who is that man?" I asked.

"An Irishman," Nils answered, "a member of the British colony in Petersburg."

"But why is he here?"

"I guess he'll be taking care of Georges . . . now that Grandmother's gone. Last night I overheard Father telling Uncle Kolya that Mr. Boyle was highly recommended by some of Mother's Christian Science friends."

"Well, I don't like this Mr. Boyle."

"Don't worry. We won't be seeing much of him."

"Why not?"

"Because Mr. Boyle and Georges will stay out on Kamenny Ostrov. Father said so." Nils was referring to our suburban villa.

We dropped the subject, and for some months I thought no more of Mr. Boyle. Then summer came, and, since Vasilievskoye had been sold, we went to a seaside resort in Estonia, a place on the Baltic Sea called Hapsal. Father had rented an attractive house right on the water. It had a comfortable porch, a library, even a billiard room. There was a guest cottage for Georges and Mr. Boyle. In the main house the stairs above the second floor led to a glassed-in cupola overlooking a shady garden and a small jetty going out into the bay. Several canoes and a rowboat were tied up at the jetty.

The canoes immediately caught my eye. They promised an exciting new pastime. I found two old umbrellas in the house. This discovery gave me an idea that I promptly put into action. Whenever the breeze blew from off the sea, I paddled out in one of the canoes. I would go almost a mile out into the bay before I turned the canoe around. Then I would open

the umbrellas and coast to the shore, using them as sails. I
was delighted with my new exploit, my first adventure in the
open sea.

One day when I was out in the bay, the wind shifted and,
hard as I tried, I could not row myself back. Mr. Boyle, who
had been watching from the shore, came to get me. How
humiliating! What was worse, when Mother heard about it
she said I absolutely could not go out into the bay alone unless I learned to swim. She thought that Mr. Boyle would be
only too glad to teach me. She was quite adamant about it. I
was eleven at the time.

Learning how to swim from Mr. Boyle did not appeal to
me. Granted that he was good for Georges as Mother
claimed, there was something about him, a certain callous
quality, I did not like; and I distrusted his bland reserve. His
heartiness seemed fake. Even the way he walked bothered
me—I don't know why. Besides, I well remembered the un-
pleasantness of our first meeting. Still, I was eager to go out
in the canoe, and so I said to Mother, yes, I would like to
learn to swim if Mr. Boyle would teach me.

I soon regretted that decision. Mr. Boyle's method of teaching me was simple. He took me to a bathhouse at the end of a
long jetty, and when we had put on our bathing trunks, he
simply dumped me in. "Sink or swim," he said as I splut-
tered and struggled in the water. When it appeared that I
might sink, Mr. Boyle reached in and hauled me out. He allowed me a minute or two to recover, then pushed me in
again, ignoring my protests. Finally, unable to stand this tor-
ment any longer, I bolted from the bathhouse, ran home, and
raced up the stairs, all the way to the cupola. Once inside, I
locked the door behind me. Only then did I realize that I still
had on my bathing trunks, dripping wet.

Minutes later I saw the doorknob move. Then a familiar
voice said, "Open the door." I did not answer. I wanted to

shout: "You tyrant, you miserable creature," but said nothing. Mr. Boyle would not have understood my Russian, and I could not think of the right words in English. All I could do was stand there listening and clenching my fists. In my frustration, I pulled out a nail in the wall and bent it double. And as I stood there, I heard Mr. Boyle pull up a chair at the top of the stairs and settle down to wait.

Hours went by and evening came, and then a thunderstorm broke overhead. The wind tore at the window frames, and a torrent of rain engulfed the house. It was the lightning, though, flashing almost incessantly, that scared me most. I felt exposed and trapped. I crouched in the far corner of the cupola more and more anxious with every clap of thunder. But frightened as I was, I held my ground. I told myself I would not open the door and give that bully any satisfaction. Darkness came, and presently the storm subsided; and I heard Mr. Boyle go down the stairs, presumably for supper. After a while I unlocked the door and, taking every precaution not to be heard, tiptoed to my room and went to bed.

I felt abused and hungry and very angry—angry not only with Mr. Boyle, but also with Mother for letting him, as I thought at the time, bedevil me. I wanted to complain to Father, but he was far away.

Fortunately, the summer was by then nearly over. When we returned to the city, Mr. Boyle went to live with Georges in the suburban villa. I hoped I would never have anything to do with him again. I was mistaken.

During our summer in Estonia, Father had been off with the Tsar in the Black Sea. The very week of the incident with Mr. Boyle, we all had been thrilled to receive the first message that had ever come to us over the wireless. Father had sent it to us from the Tsar's yacht!

After the death of the Tsar's uncle, Father's career had taken an upturn. From his position as aide-de-camp to Grand Duke

Mikhail Nikolayevich, he had gone on to become aide to the
Tsar, a post known as *fligel adjutant.* "To receive so rare an appointment delighted me," he says in his memoirs. He goes on
to describe his first tour of duty:

. . . Quickly I arranged to have my uniform altered, and went the
following day to present myself to the Tsar and Her Majesty. . . . [They] received me most cordially, and said they were glad
that I would be a member of the suite since they had both known me
well for a long time.

A few days after my appointment I was assigned to a tour of duty.
I entered my new duties not without pleasurable emotions, leaving
for Tsarskoye Selo on the 10 o'clock train. Waiting for me at the station was a troika with three magnificent horses. It brought me
quickly to the Aleksander Palace.

I took over my duties in the quarters set aside for the duty officer
and at once proceeded to the reception rooms where ministers and
other personages were already waiting for an audience. Here too I
found the *skorokhod,* a minor court official who briefed me on the
day's program. Without him it would be difficult, for he is the expert
on court procedures and etiquette, knows everything, and alerts one
in good time about all kinds of forthcoming events. . . .

For the evening meal I was invited to the Imperial table, and it was
flattering . . . for it is not all *fligel adjutants* by any means who are
honored with an invitation to have dinner in the Tsar's family circle. . . . At the table were the Tsar and the children, while the Empress ate reclining on a couch and was alone in having a special veg-
etarian menu.

It is interesting to be at the dinner table in such rare surroundings,
forgetting entirely the honor of which one is the recipient, and observe the Imperial family's unconstrained relations: the casual conversation, simplicity and cordiality—this is the impression that remains. . . .

Service as duty officer did not come often because soon the people
at the Chancellery noticed that I enjoyed the special good graces of
the Tsar, so that my turn to serve was skipped when it fell on days

involving interesting events, especially when there were trips to the Crimea in prospect and only certain officers were assigned. Still, there always seem to be intrigues at any Court and also an abominable disease—envy.

Nevertheless, the Tsar preferred to have Father and arranged for him to go on several trips to the Crimea and to the coast of Finland. The fact is that the Tsar felt at ease with him. Father was companionable and quite a raconteur. Besides, the Tsar knew that Father would not overstep his role as military aide, would not introduce politics or controversial topics into the conversation.

Father's next promotion came four years later. He reports that

On the 2nd of January, 1914, in Tsarskoye Selo, members of the Tsar's suite were gathered to wish their majesties a Happy New Year. At the conclusion of the ceremony, the Tsar came up to me and said: "We know you well, like you, and are used to you, so I'm naming you commander of my *Konvoy*, and raising you to the rank of major general with appointment to the suite." I cannot express my joy at the unexpected appointment. There was no end of the congratulations I received, but not all by far were sincere. Especially offended was the commander of a Cossack regiment who considered himself candidate for the post.

The *Konvoy* was an elite Cossack regiment, recruited from among the most outstanding men among the Cossack troops. It had been organized a hundred years earlier to guard Tsar Alexander I during the war against Napoleon. In recent times the duty of protecting the Tsar had been taken over largely by the Secret Service, and the *Konvoy* served primarily as a military escort, fulfilling a ceremonial role of accompanying the Tsar. But it continued to come directly under the Tsar's authority through the Minister of Court, and Father, therefore, had

no other military superior, a unique status. During the World
War I various sections of the *Konvoy* served in different loca-
tions. One contingent was always with the Tsar at General
Headquarters; another was stationed at Tsarskoye Selo with
the Empress; a third was at the front, rotating with the other
sections; the balance was quartered at the capital.

"I've always wanted to be free of meddling superiors,"
Father told us, "and now it's come to pass." However ironic
his comment proved in the light of history, he was not exag-
gerating. Only a few military men in Russia enjoyed so enviable a position.

A parade of the *Konvoy* was scheduled about six months
after Father's appointment, and he arranged for Nils and me
to attend. I have some vivid memories of the occasion: the
large palace courtyard at Tsarskoye Selo lined with *Konvoy*
Cossacks in red parade uniform and mounted on splendid
steeds. Their tall hats of black Persian lamb—*papakhas*—added
to their imposing stature. The Empress and her daughters on
the steps leading to the palace; a little to one side, a group of
notables. Among them, very overawed, Nils and I—all waiting for the Tsar to come to the reviewing stand.

Then, as everyone waited, our ears caught a faint sound as
of surf on a distant shore. The sound mounted, and soon we
could hear the voices of hundreds of civilians and soldiers
who lined the road to the royal palace all shouting *"Urra-a-a-
h!"* as the Tsar drove by in his Delaunay-Belleville. The sound
grew to a roar as the imperial car entered the courtyard.

I had never seen the Tsar that close before, nor the
Tsarevich. They were both dressed for the occasion in *Konvoy*
uniform.

The car stopped. The Tsar stepped out. While the Tsarevich
was helped to his mother's side, the Tsar mounted a handsome stallion and placed himself *en face* the assembled regiment ranged around the courtyard.

And then commands rang out. Column by column, the *Konvoy* wheeled to the right and circled the courtyard. As it reached the extreme left of the Tsar, it reformed in columns of some twenty abreast, each column led by an officer, and moved forward past the Tsar and the Reviewing stand.

Leading them all was Father astride a white horse and holding a bared sword. As the first column approached the Tsar, Father spurred his horse into a gallop and, executing a semicircle, took a position next to the Tsar. And then the whole regiment passed in review.

I held my breath as Father performed the maneuver; Nils gripped my arm. We were both thrilled to see Father leading the regiment. It was the first time in my life I had seen him in his military role.

No one in all of Russia had a dress uniform exactly like his. It was a scarlet tunic embroidered in gold. At his belt he wore a gold dagger, a gift from the Tsar. On his chest were various decorations: the Cross of Saint Vladimir; the French Legion of Honor; Bokhara's Gold Star; also, on his left side, the white Maltese Cross of a Corps des Pages graduate. In his senior year he had been outstanding and so was chosen *page de chambre*, which is to say that he was to serve that year as page to a member of the Imperial family during ceremonial occasions. The pages so honored came to be known at Court.

When we went to the theater, everyone looked at Father as we came in. I was proud to be his son.

There was no doubt that Father had achieved an enviable position. But it was not an altogether happy turn of events for Nils and me. We saw Father less than ever. His duties kept him constantly busy. And, as the tension prior to World War I increased, his schedule at Court became all the more demanding.

That summer a number of official visitors arrived in Russia.

The Tsar received these foreign notables at Peterhof, a palace on the Gulf of Finland. A bungalow near the palace was placed at Father's disposal for the duration of the state visits. Our entire family, including Georges and, alas, Mr. Boyle, joined Father there.

The first official visitor after our arrival was Admiral Beatty of Great Britain. As a gesture of Great Britain's solidarity with Russia, he brought the First Battle Cruiser Squadron of the Royal Navy to St. Petersburg. The Tsar entertained him, and he, in turn, entertained the Tsar at a luncheon on his flagship, H.M.S. *Lion,* where Father met the admiral.

The next to come was President Poincaré of France, his visit another gesture of Allied unity. Escorting the French president, Father rode at the head of a detachment of *Konvoy* Cossacks, just behind the carriage in which the Tsar brought the president of France to the palace. To me this was a most impressive ceremonial occasion.

I was twelve-and-a-half years old, but still too young to grasp the significance of these state visits. Quite unconcerned, I spent my time at Peterhof bicycling around the palace grounds, occasionally sitting on a bench to admire the spectacular fountains. I also went bathing in the Gulf of Finland, played tennis with officers of the *Konvoy*, and took walks with Nils.

The final clash between Mr. Boyle and me came while we were still in Peterhof. Father had gone on a brief cruise with the Tsar and Mother had taken the occasion to visit a friend at Tsarskoye Selo, some twenty miles away. During her absence she left Mr. Boyle in charge of the household. I only learned of this arrangement after she had left, and I immediately felt threatened. But there seemed to be nothing to do about it.

I was even more concerned when I learned that Mother—without telling me—had left instructions for Mr. Boyle to give me dictation in Russian while she was away. Mr. Boyle could hardly speak Russian at all. His accent had the effect of doubling my spelling errors. Then he made me copy each misspelled word twenty-five times. But that was nothing compared with other tyrannies yet to come.

As it happened, Mr. Boyle was a health faddist. As soon as Mother left, he introduced a new regime. Every night before I went to bed, he fetched a dishpan filled with ice-cold water and made me put my feet in it. "Everyone," he said, "should build up his physique and harden himself." The first two nights I put up with his sadistic whim, but the third night I balked: I refused to put my feet into that cold water any more. I wished I could call on Nils for help, but he was away observing one of the patriotic rallies that were held on the eve of World War I.

"Oh-h-h-h!" drawled Mr. Boyle. "You won't, you say?"

"I won't."

"Well, in that case, I'll have to punish you."

This said, he seized me by the shoulders and jerked me forward until I fell across his knees. He reached for a cane, which he apparently had readied for the purpose, and gave me a resounding whack with it. Indignant, I let out a yell. No one had ever laid hands on me before, and no one ever would again, I swore. My loud yell must have startled Mr. Boyle because he loosened his hold on me.

That momentary lapse was all I needed; I wriggled out of his grasp and ran. I ran straight to Father's room and opened his desk drawer, where I knew he kept his service revolver. Seizing the gun in both hands, I pointed it at Mr. Boyle, who had followed me into the room.

"Don't you come any closer!" I panted.

"Put down that gun," he said, but stopped on the threshold.

"You touch me, and I'll kill you!" I shouted.

We stood facing each other in complete silence—five, ten,

fifteen minutes. The situation was becoming more and more grotesque. It couldn't last. By then I had calmed down somewhat and knew I wouldn't pull the trigger, though I might have hit him with the butt if he had came close. Fortunately, Mr. Boyle reconsidered. He turned on his heels and left the room.

When Father and Mother returned, they had a long conference with Mr. Boyle, and then they called me in. They both looked pained, and Father said that he was sorry to hear about my bad behavior; and he went on to tell me that he and Mother had decided on a punishment for me. I would be sent to school at once—that is, starting in the fall. I was still too young to enter the Corps des Pages at which I was already enrolled for the following year. During the intervening year, I would be sent to a less exclusive military school. This step was being taken, Father added gravely, because it was apparent that I did not know how to behave myself at home.

10

JUGGLER IN THE NIGHT

"What did you expect?" asked Nils when I complained that I did not like the Aleksandrovsky Kadetsky Korpus. "After all, it is not the Corps des Pages." I hadn't known what to expect. I hadn't been to school before.

The Aleksandrovsky Kadetsky Korpus, though not renowned, was considered a good school. It prepared boys for service as officers in the regular Russian army. Yet somehow I felt uncomfortable there. Nils pointed out that most of the boys came from a less privileged background. That, he said, explained my difficulties. As usual, he was right. As soon as my classmates became aware of Father's position at court and my occasional arrival at school with car and chauffeur, they kept their distance. Not that they were unfriendly; still, differences in status and worldly goods got in our way. I felt isolated.

One bright spot was French class. The French teacher and I got on well together. I was the only boy who already spoke the language. He liked to chat with me in French. It's not surprising that the others looked on me as teacher's pet. Monsieur Flaubert was a roundish little man. His pale, gray eyes peered over his spectacles with a benign and wistful look.

"*C'est un nom célèbre,*" he would announce proudly as he paced up and down the classroom. It may have been a famous name in France, but not one of us had ever heard of it. To remind himself of his name seemed to bolster him. I wondered what had brought him all the way to Russia in the first place.

"*Préférez-vous vivre içi plutôt qu'en France?*" I once inquired.

"*Oui, je préfère vivre içi,*" he answered not too enthusiastically. And I still wondered. What mattered was that there was a bond between us, perhaps because we both were lonely.

When I learned one day that he was ill, I was concerned. When he did not appear for several days, I decided to call on him and bring him a present to cheer him up. With three rubles I had saved, I went to Eliseeff's, the best food store in town, and bought a large chocolate cake of a kind I particularly liked. Clutching the package in one hand and a scrap of paper with his address on it in the other, I took a streetcar and set out to visit him.

He lived on Vasilievsky Ostrov in a drab section of the city. After a search, I located the right street and the right house number. I found that my teacher lived on the third floor. When I had climbed three flights of stairs, I came to his living quarters. The entrance door was ajar. I knocked. There was no answer, so I walked in. He lived in two dingy rooms. Clothes, books, and dishes were scattered about. Monsieur Flaubert himself was lying on the bed. He wore a pink bathrobe. His face was flushed, his hair rumpled.

He seemed surprised to see me. "Oh, it's you," he said, looking up at me with those now feverish gray eyes. "Don't come too close. I must have quite a temperature."

"I've brought you a cake," I said as I put the box down on a small table. "I got it specially for you. I hope you'll like it."

"Thank you. Thank you so much," he answered. He smiled graciously and raised himself on the bed. I could see it took effort. "And now you'd better go. . . ."

"I hope you'll be well soon. How do you feel?"

"Not so good."

"What does the doctor say? Have you seen one?"

"Not yet, but one is coming . . . You'd better go," he said again. "I really feel quite ill and what I have may be contagious."

For a few seconds I stood on the threshold, reluctant to leave, not knowing what to say. "Get well soon," I repeated, and turned and left.

A week went by and then it was announced in school that we were soon to have a new French teacher. Monsieur Flaubert, I learned, had been ill with diphtheria. Taken to the hospital, he had died there a few days later.

I reacted to the news of my teacher's death with dismay and sorrow, but went on about my business as usual. That was a gloomy time in my life. I was just beginning to be used to going to school every morning in the dark. I could scarcely see the streetcar. During the winter months it didn't get light in St. Petersburg until midmorning. Surprisingly, Russia's old capital is in about the same latitude as Anchorage, Alaska.

Not long after Monsieur Flaubert's death, I learned that the mark I had received for good behavior had been lowered. Why, I asked, had my report card been changed? I had been very proud to get such a high mark. The homeroom teacher didn't know why. Nobody seemed to know. When I took my woes to Nils, he told me he had overheard a telephone conversation between Mother and someone at my school. Nils was quite sure he heard Mother say she found it odd that I had been given such a high mark for good behavior. "Undoubtedly an error—he is so ill-behaved at home."

A few days later I lost my voice in choral class. Until then, group singing had been one of my favorite activities at school. But suddenly I'd open my mouth to sing and an unfamiliar sound would come out.

Also about then I found I could no longer digest my lunches. The food served at school revolted me. I couldn't touch it. At home, too, whatever I ate upset me. Mother called the doctor. He poked about my stomach and shook his head. He finally prescribed a daily enema with warm oil. Maybe he did not completely overlook the emotional factors, for he added, "And perhaps he should have his lunches somewhere else." Fortunately, Ella Grabbe Pahlen, a newly married cousin of mine whom I liked, lived near the school. She agreed to have me come for lunch every day. I liked going to her apartment; she was so kind and understanding, and her lunches were delicious!

One day Cousin Ella took me to a matinee performance of the circus. We both enjoyed our afternoon together. She especially liked the French poodles that jumped through white paper hoops. What I liked best was the juggling. Rossi, an Italian juggler, threw five, seven, and finally nine plates into the air—and kept them all moving at once—and caught them all. I was amazed and fascinated.

When I got home I looked around for some old tennis balls and that night began to practice throwing them into the air— first one, then two, and eventually three. After a while my juggling improved. The only time I practiced was at night after everyone else had gone to bed. I didn't even show my valet, Matvei, until I had perfected my juggling. He was impressed, and I was delighted with my new skill. Here was something no one else in the family could do, not even Nils.

"That's quite a trick!" Nils exclaimed with surprise as he

watched me toss three oranges into the air—one right after the other—and juggle them smoothly. I knew he meant it; he could never juggle, not even if he tried.

My spirits rose, and soon my health improved. Nevertheless, I was relieved when spring came and school was over. In the fall I'd be going to the Corps des Pages.

Meanwhile, I had developed another interest. In a magazine I had read an article about perpetual motion: people throughout the ages had tried to devise a mechanism that would run indefinitely on its own momentum. The idea intrigued me. It got me started on an experiment.

We had recently moved to a new apartment provided for Father by the Crown. Located in the barracks of the *Konvoy* regiment, it overlooked the Neva River. In an unused guest room I rigged up quite a contraption. A marble ran along a trough that I had fastened to the wall. Lower and lower around the room the marble went until it reached the floor. One way to prolong its motion, I figured, would be to raise its starting point. But since the starting point could not be raised indefinitely except in theory—it was the ceiling that stopped me—I tried a different approach. I found that I could prolong the motion of the marble by minimizing its loss of height as it rolled down the trough. This I accomplished when I made it run down one slope and up another, and down and up again continuously. At this critical juncture I had to interrupt what I was doing to concentrate on getting ready for the Corps des Pages entrance examinations.

Several days passed. When I went back, eager to complete my experiment, I found that someone had cleared the guest room and replaced the furniture as it had been before. A chambermaid told me that Mother had ordered her to straighten the room. She quoted Mother as saying that this was a guest room, not a playroom.

I did not show my disappointment; I wouldn't give Mother

the satisfaction of finding out how important the project had been to me. Instead, I told myself that I was relieved not to have to go on with the experiment; it would probably lead to a dead end anyway, I told myself. I pretended I didn't care.

At about the same time, I found I could not bear to hear Mother clear her throat in the morning. The sound was physically painful to me, at times almost unendurable. I could hear it distinctly. There, in the barracks apartment to which we had moved, my bed was against the wall adjoining Mother's bedroom. My extreme reaction persisted until June when we left for the country, where I lived in another part of the house. Not until September when we returned to town did my revulsion reappear, by then in a milder form. The distraction of getting adjusted to my new school must have helped.

In telling of the painful events that took place when I was twelve—school presented to me as punishment, the lowering of the grade for good behavior, destruction of my experiment in perpetual motion—it is not my intention to indict my mother or her world, only to record what happened. Nonetheless, I cannot disingenuously pretend that a mother's aggressions do not scar her children.

All the more am I grateful to Cousin Ella for her kindness. Also, perhaps, to Signor Rossi. My new-found skill as a juggler gave me the confidence I badly needed, but at a price: I came to think I had to juggle to gain acceptance—and love. The uncertainties of life after the Revolution only served to reinforce this pattern. Now I can understand why, sixty years later, Hansi Bohm put a Harlequin-patterned background in the portrait she painted of me recently. Hansi was able to perceive the conjurer there in the background.

11

THE CORPS DES PAGES

When I entered the Corps des Pages, I had no idea what a special school it was. Over the years, twelve members of Father's family had attended the Corps. I was the thirteenth. Father wanted Nils to go there, too, but Mother insisted that Nils attend the Imperial Aleksander Lycée where her brother, Uncle Kolya, had gone. At the Lycée boys were prepared for careers in diplomacy and other government service.

In my class at the Corps, two-thirds of us were day students; the rest were boarders. Most were about my age—thirteen—and came from a milieu comparable to my own. This similarity of background was no accident. To qualify for admission, a boy had to be the son or grandson of a general or civil servant of high rank. He was commissioned an officer after seven years of study and usually entered the Imperial Guard, the elite corps of the Russian army. But first, the graduate had to apply to the regiment of his choice and be accepted by its officers. This judgment was based on the personality, family background, and character of the candidate, determined in part by his reputation at school. If, for instance, he was known to be a tattler, few guard regiments would take him.

The Corps was closely linked with the Imperial household. Each year several outstanding pupils of the graduating class were selected as *pages de chambre* and attached to various members of the Imperial family whom they escorted on ceremonial occasions. Father was so chosen when he was at the Corps and thus was given the opportunity to make personal contact with the Imperial family.

The school was located in the very center of the capital, around the corner from the Nevsky Prospect. It occupied the Vorontsov Palace, given to the Corps by the Tsar in the 1820s. The building had previously been the headquarters of the Knights of Saint John after they were driven from Malta by Bonaparte. The svelte white cross of the Knights of Malta became the insignia of the Corps.

The three-story palace was handsome in an old-fashioned way, spacious and imposing. The halls were larger than a school requires—one was used exclusively for dancing class. Though the school was in the center of the city, it had a large garden with tall, old trees and paths where we younger boys romped in the half-hour recess after lunch. The three lower forms—third, fourth and fifth—occupied the top floor of one wing.

Our classrooms opened on an assembly hall into which the boys were disgorged every fifty minutes for a ten-minute break. During these recesses there was bedlam with boys running, wrestling and shouting. From a small room strategically placed at the end of the hall a duty officer watched. On the floor below, in a similar layout, were the classrooms of the older boys. We sometimes passed them on our way to lunch and eyed them speculatively. They always marched in perfect formation. We didn't.

The school chapel was large enough to permit all five of the lower forms to attend at the same time. There we stood during service, silently resigned and bored. One occasion stands out in my memory. On that day, for some reason, the priest was assisted by a substitute deacon, a figure so comic—recalling to me even then Chaliapin's Don Basilio in *The Barber of Seville*—that some of the boys began to titter. The sound spread, grew and soon all the boys were laughing. The service was stopped. We were marched out of the chapel and lined up, apprehensive and glum, in one of the barn-like adjoining halls. Back and forth in front of us General Rittikh, the Deputy Director, stumped nervously, trying to shame us and threatening severe punishment if the incident recurred. We heeded his warning. There was no more laughter during service. But the chapel had lost its awe and when discipline broke down after the Revolution, some of us used it as a good place to hide from the school authorities. Nobody would ever find us under the altar table with its heavy cover of velvet.

Educated at the Corps were the sons of prominent Russian families as well as those of Eastern Europe, the Middle East and Asia, including royalty. Among the distinguished graduates was the famous anarchist, Prince Peter Kropotkin, whose *Memoirs of a Revolutionist* describes the school at some length. Apparently it did not change much in fifty-eight years. Kropotkin was first in his graduating class and *page de chambre* to the Emperor himself—Emperor Alexander II—whom he got to know well, perhaps too well.

In 1915, sixteen of us entered the lowest grade. We did not stay together long—only two years. The Revolution scattered us, and we lost track of each other. Many must have perished in the Civil War. So far as I know, only one, Vasili Shulga, is still in Russia, but I am not in touch with him. Several escaped to Paris. On a recent trip I saw two of my classmates there. Maxime Kovalevsky, mathematician and retired insurance executive, is now active composing church music. He also leads a choir at l'Eglise Irenée on the Boulevard Blanqui. Count Andrei Lanskoy made a name for himself in the art world of France. In his middle sixties he won a national contest to design mosaics for the new Hall of Science at the University of Rennes.

Few have fared so well. Nikita Crichton is one of those who have suffered unduly. I saw him recently for the first time in sixty years. We sat in the waiting room of Grand Central Terminal and talked. He told me he had served in the White Army, was then imprisoned in Odessa. Later he made his way to Yugoslavia. He thought he was safe there. For a time he was safe. Then, in the chaotic conditions that came to the Balkans in World War II, he chose to join the anti-Soviet forces of the former Soviet General A. A. Vlasov—a fateful decision, for he was among those forcibly repatriated by the Allies. Tried and sentenced by a Soviet court, he spent thirteen years in a labor camp in the Far North of Russia. On his release he had to serve an additional five years as a "voluntary settler" in the region. He said the summer there was very hot, very short; the winter, very cold, very long. Under Khrushchev's more lenient regime he emigrated to the United States. Now he lives in Brooklyn on Social Security and earns an additional forty dollars a month assisting stamp collectors. At the Corps jovial Nikita sat not three feet away from me. We used to pass funny little notes to each other on scraps of white paper. Nikita is of Scottish ancestry. The ruins of Chrichton Castle still stand just south of Edinburgh.

Another classmate, Count Nikolai Rebinder—a quiet, pensive boy, as I remember him—ended his life after many attempts to adjust. Like many other Russian emigrés, he was last employed as a taxi driver in Paris.

My closest friend at the Corps, round-faced, quick-moving Paul Orlov, nicknamed "Bullet," died of tuberculosis in

France while still in his twenties before a cure had been
found for the disease.

Nikita told me that we have another classmate in the United
States. He is Nikolai Obruchev, who lives in California and
is part of a Russian religious community in San Diego.

What has become of the others? I don't know. The Revolution dropped a curtain on this period of my life and that of
my classmates. Our urgent new concern to get on in a strange
world outside Russia took all we had to give for many years.

When I entered the Corps I had to work very hard at first. I
was not too well prepared. We studied Russian, French, and
German, geography, geology, physics, geometry, and arith-
metic. Of course we had gymnastics and military drill. We
also had religious studies in which we read the Bible. The
subjects I liked best were Russian and geography. In both we
had outstanding teachers.

Valentin Mikhailovich Pushin taught us the Russian language and Russian literature. As I remember him, he was a
man of massive frame, slow-moving and slightly stooped.
Promptly at ten he lumbered into our classroom and lowered
himself ponderously into his chair. "Good morning," he
mumbled vaguely as his nearsighted eyes searched his desk.
From an inner pocket he produced a pencil and a black
notebook, and busied himself scribbling something down. We
would wait, watching silently, while he continued to write.
Professor Pushin was never in a hurry.

Then suddenly he would look up and start to talk. Immediately he would be transformed. His eyes shone, his features came alive, and the emotion in his voice commanded
our attention. Some of the time he would read to us passages
from the Russian classics. Through him I became aware of
Pushkin's felicitous use of the Russian language, of the strong
and weak points in Gogol's style. I liked Valentin

Mikhailovich, looked forward to his classes. He stimulated me to read; and thanks to Nils, who had accumulated a sizable library, I read through most of Pushkin, Chekhov, and Turgenev by the time I was fifteen.

The other teacher I remember well was Staff Captain Boris Ivanovich Chizhov. His subject was geography. A wiry, nervous man in his mid-thirties, Captain Chizhov strode around our classroom gesturing and talking. What he had in common with Professor Pushin was his dedication to his subject. Frequently he unrolled a map on the blackboard, pointed to an area, and called on us to tell him something about its physical characteristics, climate, and natural resources. He asked us to describe the people who lived there. What are they like, he'd say? How do they live? What do they do? And what do they believe? Often without waiting for an answer, he would launch himself on an exciting lecture and answer his own questions. Almost invariably he broke through our indifference.

I admired Captain Chizhov so much that halfway through the school year I took up a collection among my classmates and got him a small Easter egg from Fabergé. We solemnly presented it to him in class. "Why, that's really wonderful," he said, surprised and pleased. "I'll wear it on my watch chain."

I did not know how lucky I was to have such good teachers. Had I known, I might not have listened to my cousin, Nika Grabbe, a recent graduate. One day he took me aside and said, "Listen, Pavlik. You don't have to work so hard in school. Grades aren't that important. It's better to be sociable than studious. The school will graduate you regardless of your marks."

Nika was a glamorous officer in the Horse Guards—tall, dashing, and handsome. I liked him. I was impressed by what he said. Immediately, my grades declined. As I was about to fail my course in Russian history, I made an eleventh-hour attempt to pass the examination. The night before, I stayed up very late and memorized 120 dates. The next day, when I appeared before the three teachers who were my examiners, I answered every question correctly. One of the teachers, an older man with a flowing-white beard, finally shook his head. "Your past record," he said, clearing his throat and stroking his beard, "couldn't be worse. Yet your answers are correct. I feel there's something wrong, though I don't know what it is." He then conferred with his colleagues and gave me a barely passing grade.

This incident discouraged me further. My marks sank to a new low.

Paradoxically, my low marks enhanced by standing with my classmates. They all despised *zubrílas*—greasy grinds—and looked up to boys who were athletic or showed initiative in the affairs of the group. I fitted into the latter category. An unexpected incident further enhanced my standing.

One fine spring day I noticed a ledge outside our classroom window, just wide enough to walk on. I opened the window and climbed out. Soon I found myself on the roof of the building. Glancing below, I caught sight of our homeroom teacher, Lieutenant Colonel Zarzhevski, meeting an attractive blonde. The colonel was short and plump and very strict. I rushed back to our classroom, rounded up some classmates, and led them to the roof. From there we watched the colonel, smiling and gesturing, escort his lady friend through the gate of the school and out into the street.

Up until then we had all suffered Colonel Zarzhevski's harsh discipline. Now he suddenly changed, after some of us dropped a hint or two.

While I felt congenial with the other boys, I couldn't share their enthusiasm for military matters. Parades, uniforms, and decorations fascinated them. They looked down on service in the regular army as somehow demeaning. I could not care less about the relative merits of this or that regiment, and I especially disliked military drill.

This aversion I associate with visits to our home during my childhood of Vladimir Nikolayevich Voyeikov, husband of Mother's best friend, Nini, *née* Fredericks. At that time he was a colonel in the Imperial Hussars. Mother had bought replicas of his regiment's uniform, which Nils and I were made to wear during his visits.

When Colonel Voyeikov appeared we were instructed to put on the uniform and summoned to the living room. I must have been five or six at the time. A swashbuckling figure, the colonel delighted in ordering us about. Sternly, he lined us up and put us through various forms of marching drill. I can still hear his threatening voice bellowing out orders. I hated him with all my heart. Nils did, too. Incidentally, he never came when Father was home. Though they were Corps des Pages classmates, Father didn't like him, found him arrogant. *"Nesterpimy"*—"insufferable"—was the word he used. Yet there was no way for Father to prevent his visits.

Thanks, no doubt, to Colonel Voyeikov, my dislike of military drill carried over to the early days at the Corps. Colonel Zarzhevski had a hard time teaching me how to salute or stand at attention. For the first month or two, in fact, I was not permitted to wear the school's uniform because of my unmilitary posture. "Didn't I want to be an officer?" my homeroom teacher asked despairingly. "Not necessarily," I mused. I had decided not to remain an officer beyond the years required for military service. To special friends I confided that I might become a traveling bishop, a fancy I had picked up somewhere, and spend my life visiting the oppressed and dispossessed around the world.

Hazing was another aspect of school life on which I did not

see eye-to-eye with my classmates. From the moment I entered the school, the upper classmen saw in me a likely prospect. At the Corps, hazing was a tradition. Perhaps my posture indicated all too clearly that I was not the ideal candidate for the military life they so admired. They'd show me! They ordered me to recite their names in alphabetical order or in a special sequence that they revised each week. I also had to name the regiments of the Imperial Guard and describe their uniforms; or I was asked questions relating to the military tradition. If I made the slightest error, they made me stand at attention in the lavatory, do sitting-up exercises, remain motionless during recess, or refrain from speaking to my classmates. My friend, Rebinder, suffered as much, but for some reason he was able to shrug off the hazing more easily than I could.

Something had to be done. I persuaded my classmates to stage a demonstration every time one of us was victimized by the older boys. The school was supposed to be opposed to hazing, though the masters tended to look the other way. I reckoned correctly that if enough fuss was made, they would have to do something about it. After a couple of noisy encounters in which we marched around shouting in protest and stamping our feet until the duty officer rushed over to find out what was up, the older boys suddenly desisted. But, alas, when the time came later for our class to do the hazing, most of my classmates couldn't resist lording it over the younger boys.

Was this tradition of hazing comparable to the testing of baboons for acceptance into the troop? Or was it, rather, a way to build up adolescent egos that was viewed by some of the masters as desirable preparation for military command?

At home, when I mentioned my disinclination for military life, Father reminded me that I came from a military family.

His father had been a general. So had three of my great-grandfathers. I was even named for one of them, General Count Pavel Khristoforovich Grabbe. His ancestors had come from Sweden, presumably descended from a partisan of Gustav Vasa, one Nils Grabbe, who brought the Reformation to Finland. When Russia took over Finland as a grand duchy, the family became Russianized. My great-grandfather, a Lutheran, was the first Grabbe to serve in the Russian Army.

This much Father had told me, and that's all I knew for many years. Nor was I interested at that time in learning more. Then, one day in 1947, I found a new source of information as surprising as it was unexpected. While searching in the Library of Congress to see how my own books were catalogued, I came upon the listing of a book in Russian, published in 1846, and written by my great-grandfather. I called for the book. In the introduction, Pavel Khristoforovich said he had always regretted not knowing more about his forebears and so had decided to write these memoirs in the hope that his descendants might know about his life. Chance had led me to the book a century later.

That very afternoon I read my great-grandfather's memoirs from cover to cover. They gave me more of a picture of the man, his career, and his times than I had had before. Clearly, he had presence of mind and was not easily intimidated. He tells what happened when, as a young officer recently appointed military attaché, he presented his credentials to Prince Baryatinsky, Russia's envoy to Bavaria.

The butler escorted me to the English garden where we found the Prince strolling, alone. I had several packets of letters and dispatches for him, and as we met, with scarcely a word of greeting, he began reading, tearing open the envelopes and throwing them on the ground.

He was a tall, stately man with graying hair, pleasant features,

quick, impatient gestures. Apparently not everything was to his liking in the letters, particularly the relative freedom of action I was
given, independent of his control. This could be guessed from the
fact that several times he interrupted his reading and gave me a
stern, searching look.

Once he had finished reading, he inclined his head, and, pointing
with his gaze to the discarded envelopes at his feet, ordered me to
pick them up to see if they were empty. I knew the moment was
decisive. Meeting his gaze for a second, I turned my head toward the
butler who had remained standing a short distance away, and
motioned to him to pick up the envelopes. Not a word was spoken
as we watched the butler hastily gather up the pieces of paper. But
this quick, silent exchange was sufficient to establish our future relations. From that point on they became and remained most cordial.

Evidence of Pavel Khristoforovich's independence of mind
occurred when Napoleon invaded Russia. He had been recalled from Bavaria to serve under General Ermolov, who had
earlier been his commanding officer. He was then twenty-
three. As Ermolov's staff officer he was able to take part in an
historic meeting. Napoleon was at the gates of Moscow. Field
Marshal Kutuzov had called a council of war at Fily on a hill
above the city. The French historian, Alfred Rambaud,* describes the meeting: "The sight of the great and holy city extended at their feet, condemned perhaps to perish." The
question was whether to stand and fight or to retreat. Some
favored battle. Rambaud quotes "artillery officer Grabbe" as
saying, " 'It would be glorious to die under Moscow, but it is
not a question of glory.' " In making this comment, he not
only dared to oppose the advice of the illustrious General
Barclay de Tolly, but also showed his grasp of the real military
need: to keep the army intact. Even General Ermolov favored
a last battle. Kutuzov listened to all, then ordered a retreat.

*In *Russia*, vol 2, trans. Leonora B. Lang (New York: Peter Fenelon Collier,
1898), p. 183.

Reading through the memoirs of this great-grandfather there in the Library of Congress, I tried to understand the course his life had taken. He was a heroic, even a tragic figure. He took part in every military campaign that occurred in his lifetime—twenty-eight in number—and was several times wounded. Every decoration for valor was bestowed on him. He was promoted to the rank of general. And yet . . .

His espousal of liberal causes got him into serious trouble with the government. At thirty-six he was jailed for four months for associating with the Decembrists. After he reached the age of fifty-three he was out of favor with the military top command and kept without assignment for extended periods of time. Financially embarrassed, he could not afford to pay for treatment for his wife. Her nervous condition led to suicide, possibly brought on by the death of two sons in battle. At sixty-one he made this touching entry in his diary: "A letter from Paris informs me of my election as Honorary President of the International Society for the Abolition of Traffic in Negroes and Slavery. . . . Spent all day at home, ill. My old wound bleeding profusely. Lacking money to pay for the treatment, am not calling the doctor. . . ."

At long last, at the age of seventy-three, recognition came to the old soldier. He was appointed Ataman of the Don Cossacks. When he retired four years later, he was given the hereditary title of count as well as Russia's highest honor, the Order of Saint Andrew. What changes brought about this belated recognition, I don't know. I do know that Tsar Nicholas I was well disposed toward him, so it may be that his son, Aleksander II, learned from him that recognition was long overdue.

Thereafter, until his death at eighty-six, Pavel Khristoforovich lived quietly on his small estate in southwestern Russia, riding out into the open country every morning—as

Father remembers him, "a proud old man sitting erect on his horse."

If as a boy I had known this much about the man for whom I am named, I might have felt differently about a military career. The more so if I had realized that there was a great deal more involved besides marching drills, decorations, and uniforms. No one told me about military science or encouraged my proclivity for games involving strategy and planning.

I must say, though, that I came to like the Corps des Pages more and more; every morning I left home looking forward to another day at school. When my schooling was cut short by the Revolution, I was sorry to be deprived of what for me had become a haven.

Today, as in the past, the Vorontzov Palace houses a military school. The exterior of the building remains unchanged. Inside, the pictures of Imperial notables have been removed from the walls and stored in the basement. At the main gate a plaque in red-colored glass with gold letters identifies the building in Russian as the Leningrad Suvorov Military Academy. The boys are the sons of a new elite.

12

SUPPER FOR THE BISHOP

One balmy day in June 1915, Nils and I were on our way to
Bogorodskoye, Mother's small estate southeast of Moscow.
We had never summered there before. After a short drive
from the railroad junction, we entered the village of Lounino.
Ahead of us the road ended at a tall fence almost hidden from
view by a profusion of lilac bushes in full bloom. We caught a
glimpse of a gate and, beyond it, a house of pink sandstone.

"This must be it!" Nils exclaimed. "We've arrived!"

All through the journey Nils and I had wondered: what was
Bogorodskoye like? How would it compare with Vasilievskoye? And now at last we were there.

Best of all, we had come unsupervised. What excitement!
Mother had been delayed in the city. Only the French governess, Mlle. Vernier, and my new tutor, Volkov—we called
him Vladimir Aleksan'ch—had come with us. Nils and I felt
that we could cope with both of them. As it turned out, we
could. Pretty Mlle. Vernier didn't understand Russian very
well, and Vladimir Aleksan'ch—tall, dark and intense—

seemed amiable enough. He was the son of a professor. An engineering student, he had taken the job for the summer to pay for his studies. He was idealistic and forthright. I liked him immediately, and I could tell that Mlle. Vernier did, too. Whether Mother would get along with him was another question.

As our troika drove along Lounino's main street, Foma had to slow up the horses. Pigs, scraggly chickens, and small children scattered on all sides. To judge by the sagging roofs, the village was a poor one. Yet it had its own church set off by a white picket fence. In contrast to its impoverished surroundings, the church was freshly painted. So was the priest's residence.

Outside the church there was unusual activity. One peasant in a red-embroidered shirt was repairing the church steps. Another on a ladder was replacing a broken pane, and still a third was adjusting something in the belfry. Directing the work was a burly man in a dark, flowing vestment.

"He must be the priest," Nils said. "Let's ask him what's up."

Foma stopped the carriage. Nils and I got out and crossed the street.

"*Zdrastvuitye*," said Nils. "Good day to you. We've just arrived to spend the summer here, at Bogorodskoye. And you are Father . . ."

"Father Lavrenti," said the priest. "I heard that you were coming. Delighted to have you here. As you can see we're cleaning up a bit."

"Preparing for a holiday?"

"Oh, no! We're getting ready to receive His Eminence the Bishop. He's coming from Ryazan."

"You mean he's coming here?"

"Indeed he is. His yearly visit to the churches in the district. He will be here next Tuesday."

Impatient to reach the estate, we waved good-bye and climbed back into the carriage.

When we drove up to Bogorodskoye's manor house, Yegor was at the door. As usual, he and Danila had come the day before. We barely greeted them, so eager were we to explore the place.

The house was built on a bluff. There was a fine view from the terrace. Below us we could see the Oka flowing from horizon to horizon through low-lying grasslands. A major tributary of the Volga, the river joined the main stream farther east.

As Nils and I stood on the terrace admiring the view, a passenger steamer plied past us up the river. We saw it stop to let a herd of cattle swim across. The passengers crowded at the rail to watch.

Somebody had come up behind us on the terrace. In a deep voice he said, "Those cows aren't part of the estate. They belong to peasants in the village." Until then we had thought we were alone. "They'll swim back before sundown and find their way home," the man added.

He introduced himself: "Sidorov, the steward, at your service."

He was a big man with a surprisingly small head and an ingratiating manner. At once I took a dislike to him. I did not like his restless, shifting eyes, the way he gestured. He held an Irish setter on leash.

"The hunting here is very good," he said, "especially duck hunting in these marshes." He pointed to the river. "I'd like Your Excellency"—he was addressing Nils—"to be so good as to accept this little token. He is a splendid hunting dog."

"Thank you," said Nils taking the leash. "We'll let you know if there is anything we need."

Apparently Sidorov expected something more by way of thanks. He seemed abashed. He did not know that Nils's main interest in life was music and that he never used a gun, whereas I was just acquiring a taste for hunting. In any case, I was irked that he considered Nils important enough to rate a hunting dog, while I got nothing. "A stupid man," I thought.

"Here," said Nils when the steward had left. He handed me the leash. "I don't want the dog. Why don't you take it? And you can also have the shotgun Father gave me. Bring us a couple of ducks, will you, some day for supper."

"Just now," he went on with exaggerated casualness, "when we were going through the pantry, did you observe those wooden cases on the floor, next to the basement door?" He was unable to restrain an impish grin.

"Cases?"

"Yes, two cases of Mother's wine."

"I didn't notice."

"I did. You heard Father Lavrenti say that the bishop is coming. Well . . ." He paused and then still grinning he continued, "Why don't we entertain the bishop when he gets here? How's that for an idea! Invite him and the local clergy, too, for supper? We'll have Danila prepare a feast, and treat them also to some of Mother's wine."

"A marvelous idea!"

"I'm not so sure it's such a good idea," said Vladimir Aleksan'ch, who had come out on the terrace. "The supper, yes. Why not? But I don't think it would be right for you to serve your mother's wine without first asking her permission. Just think a moment. It isn't really yours to give away. It wouldn't be right. . . ."

He went on talking, but we weren't listening. We were too pleased with the idea of giving a big party for the bishop. What gave our plan its special fillip was that we had hit on a seemingly legitimate excuse for getting at Mother's wine.

The next few days went by in hasty preparation. There were conferences with Danila about the menu, the drafting of a letter of invitation to the bishop, a general tidying up.

By then we had explored every corner of the estate and had

decided that we liked it. The house was comfortable, the grounds attractive. It was the kind of place so often pictured in Turgenev's stories: a peaceful rural setting deep in the Russian countryside. There was an apple orchard here, a park, a tennis court, a quite extensive vegetable garden. We had our bicycles and riding horses. We could go swimming or fishing in the river or simply drift along in our rowboat. Nils had his piano; I had the player organ to keep me occupied on rainy days. Though the estate was smaller than Vasilievskoye, it seemed to answer all our needs. A major difference was the proximity of two villages. Lounino, the smaller of the two, was practically on our doorstep. And yet we were hardly aware of it; it was a different world.

By Monday the preparations were completed. The bishop had accepted for himself and six others.

Tuesday came, and promptly at six-thirty, as we watched from the porch, the bishop emerged from the village church and came striding toward our house. With him were Father Lavrenti, the deacon, two priests from neighboring parishes, and two strangers who looked like monks.

We greeted our guests and led them into the house. The bishop was a solidly built man in his mid-fifties, and vigorous for his age. He seemed kindly and had a dignified manner, but what was most striking about him was the benign expression that lighted up his face when he smiled. I noticed, as we seated ourselves around the supper table, that he wore suspended from a chain around his neck a simple but solid-looking silver cross and that he often reached for it as if to remind himself that, although the setting was secular, he was still a man of God.

He seemed to be in excellent spirits. He joked good-humoredly and made no secret of the fact that he was partial to good food.

Danila did not disappoint him.

We started out with *borshch* and sour cream. When all the plates were served, the bishop bent his head on his clasped hands and uttered a short prayer. "Oh, God," he spoke quite softly but distinctly, as if addressing someone beyond our hearing, "on Thee do we depend for our sustenance, and Thou givest us our food in good time . . ."

He went on speaking, and when the prayer was ended, made the sign of the cross, as did the rest of us. Yegor chose that moment to serve *piroshki*, some filled with chopped cabbage and some with *kasha*.

"Excellent *borshch*," commented the bishop.

"The *piroshki* couldn't be better," agreed Father Lavrenti.

For the next course, Yegor brought in a platter barely large enough to hold a fifteen-pound fish called *som*, caught in the Oka that day. It had the snout of a bulldog, the whiskers of a cat, and it was garnished with hard-boiled eggs, sautéed mushrooms, slices of lemon, and sprigs of parsley. A sauce béarnaise, made with tarragon, enhanced the fish. At this point Yegor uncorked some of Mother's bottles and poured the wine.

"Ahhh!" exclaimed the bishop. "How did you guess? Chateau d'Yquem! My favorite wine!"

"Delighted!" said Nils, rising. He raised his glass to offer a toast to the bishop and our other guests, and we all drank each other's health.

After the fish came roast duck served with brown rice, baked apples, and green beans. And all the time Yegor was kept busy filling the glasses. After the duck we had cucumber salad, and finally a dessert called *bombe surprise*. Danila took great pride in this dessert, which he had learned to make in France. It consisted of vanilla ice-cream in the form of a large cone. Inside, hidden from view, was shredded chocolate.

The conversation at the table never lagged. Carried on mainly by the bishop and by Nils, it ranged from a discussion of Russian country life and Tolstoy's views about religion to whether or not the *sterlet*, a species of sturgeon renowned for its caviar, could still be found in the Oka.

"I used to be an ardent fisherman myself," the bishop confided, "and I still know quite a few of the local fishermen by name."

During this conversation, the other clerics listened in respectful silence and sometimes exchanged appreciative comments about the food. Vladimir Aleksan'ch also ate in silence, as did Mlle. Vernier, who sat next to the deacon and didn't understand a word he said. Nor did I enter the conversation, except to ask Father Lavrenti about duck hunting in the area.

After supper we repaired to the living room, where coffee was served and where Nils entertained the guests by playing Chopin on the piano.

When the evening was over, Nils and I insisted that each member of the bishop's party carry away with him, "as a souvenir," an uncorked bottle of Mother's wine.

"You really didn't have to give all the wine away," my tutor remarked after the bishop and the other guests had left. "Your mother won't like that."

He was quite right. When Mother came with Georges a few days later and found that all her wine was gone, she was extremely angry and blamed Vladimir Aleksan'ch for the whole escapade. She also scolded Nils and me and told me to do penance by reading Tolstoy's *War and Peace* aloud to Vladimir Aleksan'ch every afternoon. This punishment was not too painful except that I often looked longingly through the window and wished I could be playing out-of-doors. The summer day beckoned. In later years I could never bring myself to go back to *War and Peace*.

Meanwhile, relations between Mother and my tutor had become strained. Sometimes she spoke to him quite sharply, almost as if he were a servant. She did not seem to be aware of his equivocal position in the household. He kept his dignity by managing never to talk back. I knew of this unhappy situation, and I was sorry. I realized that our escapade with the bishop had had some part in bringing it about. The fact is, I had grown very fond of Vladimir Aleksan'ch. There were so many things we liked to do together.

A favorite pastime was waiting in a rowboat near the shore until a tug with several barges came along. When they had passed, we'd row like mad to catch up with the last barge and tie our boat to the dinghy trailing behind it. Then we would spend the afternoon enjoying the fresh air, the sun, the sense of movement as we were towed upstream. Adding to our pleasure was the thought that our adventure was of our own making. We had devised this way of increasing the range of our excursions. Eventually we would untie our boat and let the current carry us back downstream. As the boat drifted back, we fished and occasionally would jump into the Oka for a swim. We planned it so we would reach home in time for supper. A wholly new kind of adventure. I think it is one of the fondest memories of my childhood.

On one of these trips we went farther upstream than usual and camped for the night out in the open. We had brought with us food and cooking equipment, some warm blankets and a small tent. That was the first time I had ever camped out.

There was also a game we played, a variant of hide-and-seek. I thought I had invented it. It went like this: on a scrap of paper I scribbled a note designating the location where I planned to leave a second note and dashed off on my bicycle to the spot indicated, usually somewhere in the park, the stables, or the garden. Vladimir Aleksan'ch would wait five minutes, then read the first note and set off after me, also on a bicycle. At the location indicated in the first note, he would find the second note, which I would have left in the hollow of a tree or under a stone, giving the location of the third note, and so on. The object of the game was for the pursuer to catch up with the pursued and for the latter to stay as long as possible one jump ahead. Vladimir Aleksan'ch got into the spirit of the game, too. At his suggestion we sometimes changed roles. He was a wonderful playmate and, as I came to know him better, a person I could thoroughly admire.

Then the blow came.

Someone told Mother's maid Emilia, who then told Mother, that my tutor had been observed in the park making love to the French *mademoiselle*. That was all Mother needed to know. Although the summer was only half over, she fired him immediately and told him to leave on the next train. I knew nothing of all this at the time, not even that Vladimir Aleksan'ch was leaving, until his suitcases were packed, the carriage ready, and he was knocking on my door to say good-bye.

Flabbergasted, I pleaded, "Do you really, really have to leave?"

"I do."

"But why? Why? Can't I persuade you to stay?"

"I'm afraid not. I have to go."

We stood there for a moment, looking at each other. I was baffled, and hurt. What else could his departure mean if not rejection? He shifted his weight to his other foot, then said, "I'm leaving, yes, unfortunately I have to leave, but before I go I have to tell you something. Well . . . I've had it on my mind. I may not have another chance."

"Have I offended you in any way?"

"Oh, no! Not at all. It has nothing to do with you." He paused. "Some of the things you do . . . I hope we're friends enough for me to be quite frank . . ."

I listened, waiting.

"For instance, this business about the wine. Giving away what isn't yours. A small matter, you may say. But is it really? And there are other things you've told me . . . pilfering candy, or sneaking into locked greenhouses, or taking loose change. Well, apparently we differ on what is right or wrong. I happen to believe that any wrong you do to others bounces back and hurts you. Is this far-fetched? A lot of words? Well, I don't think so."

I listened intently, my eyes on his bags. I was standing in the doorway and he was just outside my room.

"I have this firm belief, really an article of faith I want to share with you." He paused and drew a breath. "What I believe is this: that when you take what isn't yours, you steal part of yourself, part of your self-respect; that when you twist the truth for your own purposes you blur reality, confuse yourself—and you wind up a lesser person. Are you aware of that?

He stopped abruptly, and then went on, looking away, "Good-bye. It's time for me to go. I've talked too much already. I'm sorry, very sorry, I have to leave you. Believe me . . ."

I followed him outside. "Good-bye," I said as he stepped into the carriage. "I'm sorry, too." We both waved as he drove away. In another minute his carriage had disappeared beyond the gate.

Later that afternoon, when I pried the truth out of Emilia, I was furious and stomped up and down my room. But the anger, the hurt, stayed bottled up inside. I could not get it out.

From that day on I busied myself in various ways, mostly away from home. In the branches of a scraggly oak I built a house in which I spent hour after hour alone, just ruminating or reading the humorist Averchenko.

It was around this time that I developed a new enthusiasm—duck hunting—and found a new friend to share it with me. Fedyushkin was Father's orderly. He had a thick black beard and wore a Cossack uniform, a dagger at his belt. He looked quite fierce, but he was actually gentle and perceptive. He taught me not only how to carry a gun, but how to clean it and even how to make my own cartridges. Often, before daybreak, we rode down to the river where we dismounted and tied our horses to a tree. We crossed the river in a rowboat and walked about a mile through marshland. It was still dark when we came to a small pond. The place was alive with ducks, Fedyushkin said, hundreds of them, hidden in the reeds. There, just before dawn, there was a special stillness in the air. Even faint sounds carried great distances—the sluicing sound of oars in water; the distant jangle of cowbells; a dog's far-off bark.

As dawn neared, tinting the sky a pale orange, we crouched at the water's edge and waited. Suddenly our ears would catch the whistle of ducks in flight. In a moment they would be upon us, flying overhead. Then we would use our guns. The ducks came whizzing past so fast it took a sharp eye to bring any of them down. Fedyushkin had taught me that you never shoot a duck except on the wing. "But why?" I asked.

"Because"—he stopped to think—"Well, I suppose because it is God's creature and it is only right to give it a chance to get away."

The first time we went I had beginner's luck and bagged a dozen. Usually, there was no one else around. The war was on and with the price of powder so high, the peasants could no longer afford to hunt. At first I took Sidorov's "splendid hunting dog" along on these expeditions, but soon I gave him up. He was hopeless. At the first shot, instead of leaping forward to retrieve the bird, he fled in panic. Sidorov must have known this right along. He wasn't the sort to give away anything of value.

I would return from these hunting expeditions in the late

morning, tired but exhilarated. Usually I had a few ducks in my bag. The shortest way home led past a village.

We came that way until an unpleasant incident forced Fedyushkin and me to change our route. One day as we rode near the village, a group of peasant boys appeared unexpectedly from behind a shed. They jeered and started to throw stones. For the first time I became aware of the peasants' hostility to rich landowners—and their sons.

After each hunt I had to clean my gun. I spent part of every afternoon making cartridges for the next day's hunt. To get money for gunpowder, blank cartridges, and shot, I made an arrangement with Danila, the cook, which at first worked out to everyone's advantage. He bought from me the contents of my bag each day, and I immediately used the money to send to Moscow for more ammunition.

Then one day Mother discovered my arrangement with Danila. She was indignant and forbade him to buy anything more from me. When I came out on the porch where she sat reading, she looked up, frowning, and said, "You should be glad to contribute your bag to the household—not make some sort of commercial venture out of it."

This was all too much. Losing my tutor was injustice enough. To be deprived again so overwhelmed me that I could only stare. Without looking at Mother, I moved over to the window and put my fist through a pane of glass.

Startled, Mother said, "Did you have to do that? Have you cut yourself? Come here and let me see."

I didn't answer. Silently I showed her my bleeding hand. For a long time I had been unable to get my feelings out at all. Apparently I could only do so by hurting myself.

"Go get a bandage from Yegor," Mother ordered, recoiling from the sight of blood, "and be sure to tell him I want the pane replaced at once."

The summer ended on this discordant note.

13

COURTIER-FATHER

When we returned to Bogorodskoye the following summer I did not like the steward any better than I had the year before. Sensing my animosity, Sidorov kept out of my way. At harvest time somebody noticed that no apples were served at dinner. "Why not?" Mother asked Sidorov when he stopped by.

"There aren't any," the steward explained. "Only a few wormy ones. The trees you have here produce only every other year." Next day we took a walk in the orchard and, sure enough, there were no apples on the trees.

Several days later I made a discovery. Ivanushka, the lanky stable boy, showed me a silver ruble the steward had given him. "A birthday present?" I asked.

"No, no," Ivanushka boasted, grinning sheepishly. "Trofim Petrovich gave it to me for gathering apples in the orchard." It was Sidorov he meant. I slipped Ivanushka a coin so he'd tell me more.

"Let me show you," he said in a confidential tone and led

the way to a secluded place behind the stables. He unlocked the door of an old shed, and I looked inside. It was jammed with baskets of apples. They were the special native sour-sweet pippins we liked so much. No doubt about it.

"*Vot tak shtuka!*" I exclaimed—"Isn't that something!" I guessed that Sidorov was selling the apples in the nearest town and pocketing the money.

"He should be fired," I said to Father later that day.

To my surprise, Father was not at all perturbed. "Just a few apples," he remarked calmly, "so what's the difference? He's a good man otherwise."

Apparently, the matter ended there. Yet, during the next few days, Father spent an inordinate amount of time going over Sidorov's accounts. He found that the steward had been systematically stealing from the estate for at least a year. Finally convinced of the man's dishonesty, Father decided to get rid of him. "I'll have to let him go," he said reluctantly. And he did.

Unfortunately, instead of giving Sidorov a week's notice, he let him keep the job until the following New Year. What a mistake! Once the summer was over and we had gone back to the city, the steward disposed of everything on the estate he could lay his hands on. He found someone to buy all the remaining apples and all the vegetables and other crops. He sold the barnyard fowl, the pigs, the cows, the funny-looking goat we had nicknamed "Grishka"—even the grain stored in the bin, the lumber in the yard, some of our furniture, and a decrepit carriage you'd think no one would want. Having thus enriched himself at our expense, he vanished.

When I first learned what Sidorov had done, I was furious. What irked me most was that Father had vacillated when decisiveness had been required. Dimly I recognized the same shortcoming in myself. I, too, side-stepped unpleasant confrontations. But that was different. I was not willing to admit to such a weakness in myself. Much easier to blame Father and add this incident to my other grievances.

Perhaps the prime grievance against Father was that he was away so much. Even when he was home he didn't show much interest in our activities. Then, too, he seemed unnecessarily secretive, especially about money. Besides, his taste for light entertainment and convivial company made him seem different from Nils and me. The very things we liked he wouldn't or couldn't share with us. We liked Beethoven, but he preferred Delibes and Offenbach.

Father sometimes mentioned sailing in his conversation. He never failed to say how much he liked it. From these occasional remarks we learned that he owned a sailboat, which he kept at the Capital's Imperial Yacht Club. We gathered, too, that he considered himself quite a sailor. But neither Nils nor I had ever seen the boat. For years I thought that he couldn't be bothered to take us sailing. Now I realize that for Father the boat was in one compartment of life, while his family was in another. In his world, children stayed home with governesses. They weren't taken to the Imperial Yacht Club.

Still I wish that he had taken us. There were so few opportunities to share experiences with him. Try as I will, I can remember only two occasions when he and I were alone together. They both are happy memories. One I have described in an earlier chapter—the time he and I were in the railroad accident together. The other came early in my life when we were briefly alone in a small German spa.

I must have been eight years old at the time. We were staying in a hotel in a place called Vildbad. For some reason, Mother and Nils were not there and we were all alone, Father and I. Father had run out of cigarettes. He took a few coins from his pocket, gave them to me, and asked me to fetch him some from the store. This errand was the first I had ever run for him. How proud I was to be entrusted with my mission! I crossed the little mountain stream that ran past the hotel and followed the woodland path to the small town at the bottom of the hill. I bought the cigarettes, ran back with them, and gave Father the change. He said to me, "You did that well," and kissed me on the cheek. And then we both went walking in the woods. I was in seventh heaven!

There were occasions when Father took Nils and me and often Mother on special outings—to see the parade of the *Konvoy*, to the opera. I think with special pleasure of our visit with him aboard the Tsar's yacht, *Standart*, at the pier in Yalta. I was then about ten. The Tsar was not on board, and so we went around the ship and met some of the officers. Father showed us his cozy cabin. One of the officers brought me a pastry. It was delicious. I was particularly impressed with the mahogany paneling in the dining salon, so highly polished that it glistened. If I had been older, I would have been impressed with the sense of hushed efficiency that pervaded the yacht. Nobody lounged around; nobody was in evidence unless he was engaged in some task. "A floating palace," Nils remarked to me later. We were both delighted with our visit to the Imperial yacht. Such moments with Father were rare.

They were so rare, I held it against Father that he didn't spend more time with me during the years I was growing up. I now see he actually had no choice. Even at fourteen I was still too young to grasp the dimensions of his world of the nature of his problems at Court. He said little or nothing about them at home. Only occasionally did something happen that gave an inkling of what those problems were. Such an occasion was a conversation at our dinner table in late 1916. Uncle Sasha's erstwhile traveling companion, John Kirby, came to dinner. Mr. Kirby had by then grown affluent as a businessman—a butter baron with dealings in Canada and Denmark. He offered to transfer abroad a substantial sum of money, perhaps a quarter of a million rubles. Nobody, he said, would know it was Father's money.

"Thank you," Father replied, "but I can't do it."

"Well, if you change your mind . . ."

Later I asked Father, "Why can't you transfer money abroad?"

"It would be unpatriotic while the war is on," he answered. He added that the Tsar had told him that early in the war he had liquidated his holdings abroad and contributed them to the war effort. This information contradicts the long-rumored assertion that Romanov wealth is still stashed away in a London bank.

To transfer money abroad in wartime wasn't only unpatriotic; in Father's eyes it was disloyal. At that time Father felt a strong allegiance to the Tsar.

Then, for reasons beyond either man's control, a strain developed in Father's relationship with the Empress. In his memoirs he reports what happened. But first it might be of interest to tell in his own words how he came to know Aleksandra Feodorovna when she was still Princess Alice of Hesse-Darmstadt:

The year following the wedding of the Grand Duke Sergei Aleksandrovich to Elizaveta Feodorovna, Princess of Hesse-Darmstadt (older sister of the future Empress), her father, brother, and younger sister, Alice, came to St. Petersburg. I was then an officer in the regiment of the Guard Cossacks. At that time the fashionable sport was skating, and a select group skated by special Court permission on the ponds of the garden of the Tauride Palace. Among those who skated was the Empress, Maria Feodorovna, and many members of the Imperial family. It was here that I made the acquaintance of the Grand Duke of Hesse and his sisters. I often skated with them and they sometimes drove me home.

The Princess Alice was quite young, very pretty, slender, and rather shy. During a ball at the palace of Grand Duke Sergei Aleksandrovich, I had occasion to dance with Princess Alice. On the last day of the Mardi Gras at a ball in the Aleksander Palace at Tsarskoye Selo, I danced the mazurka with Princess Alice and was her partner for supper. The mazurka, followed by supper, was considered the most important dance of the evening. From this it is apparent that even at that time relations were cordial.

Further along in his memoirs, he made the following note about the Empress: "She was by nature nervous, shy, secretive, and could easily have seemed dry and unfriendly, and these qualities at first hampered her popularity, the more so because she was often compared with the Dowager Empress Maria Feodorovna."

For some years Father continued to get along with the Empress. The change came with the advent of Rasputin. In the fall of 1914 the Empress learned of Georges' ailment and through an intermediary suggested that it might be well for Father to meet Rasputin and ask his help. Although aware of Aleksandra Feodorovna's faith in the healing powers of the *starets* and of the possible consequences of a refusal, Father declined to see him. The risk of being tagged as someone who consorted with Rasputin was too great. The refusal resulted in an immediate cooling in Father's relationship with the Empress.

More problems developed unexpectedly for Father when Anna Virubova, close friend and confidante of the Empress, was hurt in a train accident. As he tells it:

On January 2, 1915, as a result of an employee's carelessness on the railroad to Tsarskoye Selo, there was a train wreck. Several people were killed and many wounded. Among the latter was Anna A. Virubova, who suffered fractures in both legs as she had been pinned under a derailed car. The *Konvoy* sergeant, Lazarev, hearing her moans, pulled Virubova from under the car and helped to get her to Tsarskoye Selo. The sergeant was thanked and generously rewarded. The matter seemed closed.

But no. The incident caused a complete break in my relationship with Virubova. She demanded a special promotion for Lazarov, but unfortunately it was not possible for me to grant her request because it would have gone contrary to the established order of service in the *Konvoy*, and so I had to refuse. Virubova would not listen to my explanations. She answered: "If that's the way it is, all right. Just you wait and see. You'll have reason to remember me!"

Father soon found out what a vindictive person Virubova was. She seized the first opportunity to do damage to him: she took a wholly fabricated tale to the Empress. At that time the war with Germany had been underway for two years, and Father was with the Tsar at General Headquarters in Mogilev; the Empress was at Tsarskoye Selo, and Virubova close by. Virubova reported to her that Father was using tennis as a pretext to bring the Tsar together with Mme. Soldatenko, glamorous wife of a young officer. The Empress, a very jealous woman, not only listened to the story but believed every word of it. Dismayed, she wrote to her husband at Mogilev on September 7, 1916: ". . . please don't let them present Mme. *Soldatenko* [her italics] to you—you remember I told you I had the conviction *Grabbe* wants to do it. And fancy that nasty man had the idiocy of telling Nini, his friend, that he hoped I will not be going now to *Headquarters* so as to get you acquainted with her & that she might become your mistress. . . ."*

It was not until 1933, after publication of the correspondence between the Tsar and the Empress, that Father learned Nicholas had tried to defend him against these accusations. On September 8, 1916, the Tsar wrote his wife:

What you told me yesterday of Grabbe and what he told Nini [Voyeikov] greatly surprised me. I remember some time in the sum-

The Letters of the Tsaritsa to the Tsar, 1914–1916. Introduction by Sir Bernard Pares (London: Duckworth, 1923)

mer Igor [Prince Igor Konstantinovich, cousin of the Tsar] spoke of arranging tennis here, expressing the hope that I would come and watch the play. I answered him that he should mind his own business and not interfere with other people's. The same evening at tea I was left alone with Grabbe, and he told me how right I was to refuse to visit that place, which is frequented by Mme. Soldat[enko] and other ladies, as it would probably have given rise to all sorts of absurd gossip. So I do not know how to reconcile these two facts—I mean, what Grabbe told N. and then me.

My beloved, you may be quite sure that I shall *not make her acquaintance*, whoever may wish it. But you, for your part, must not allow A. [Anna Virubova] to bother you with stupid tale-bearing—that will do no good, either to yourself or to others. . . .**

Certainly "no good" came to Father from the rumors. Despite this exchange of letters between the Empress and her husband, she apparently persuaded him to offer Father another assignment and thus to remove him from the Tsar's company. To quote Father:

The Tsar quite casually offered me the command of an army division. I thanked him but declined, saying I planned to retire soon. A few weeks later the Tsar again offered to appoint me, this time, as Ataman of the Don, a post that had meanwhile become vacant. I again declined, suggesting in my place my brother Mikhail. But this time I asked if the offer meant that the Tsar was dissatisfied with me in any respect. This he denied, assuring me that he would take my suggestion about my brother and insisting that our relations had not changed.

But I knew otherwise. I had been at Court too long not to know that anyone who incurred the disapproval of the Empress did not stay around very long.

**The Letters of the Tsar to the Tsaritsa, 1914–1917* (New York: Dodd, Mead, 1929). In 1933 a friend sent Father a Russian translation of the letter from the German edition.

What chagrin for Father to realize that the Tsar could be influenced by Virubova's vicious slander. It must have been
hard for the Tsar, too, as Father was one of the few disin-
terested people around him.

At this point Father came to see that the relationship was
no longer one of mutual trust. He was making the necessary
preparations for his retirement from the army when the Revolution intervened.

As the events relating to the Revolution and the Tsar's abdication are well known, I shall limit myself in large part to
Father's interpretation of events as reflected in his memoirs.

By March 12, 1917, a serious crisis had developed in Petrograd. In his memoirs, Father reports how events were affecting
the Tsar at general headquarters:

Mogilev, March 12, 1917. All morning we [the Tsar and his aides]
sat in the governor's palace and several times General Alekseyev
came with telegrams from Petrograd where the situation has grown
alarming during the past several days.

In the afternoon we stayed indoors waiting for more news. In the
evening Count Fredericks and Voyeikov came in while we were having tea and called the Tsar out into the adjoining room. We assumed
they wanted to tell him something particularly important as they
usually never came at night. . . . When the Tsar came back into the
dining room, it was barely noticeable that he was upset.

In about twenty minutes' time, they came again and we took our
leave, surmising that something really serious had occurred. The
fligel adjutants went to their quarters, but I waited in Dr. Feodorov's
room while he stayed upstairs in Voyeikov's quarters to find out
what was going on.

In about thirty minutes the doctor reappeared. When I asked him
what had happened, he called out to me as he passed on the run,
"Tell you later. Now you'd better pack. We're leaving in an
hour. . . ."

Hurriedly, I got my things together and went to the train. . .

With word of the uprising in the Capital, the Tsar had decided to leave at once to join his family at Tsarskoe Selo.

Father continues:

In the train we learned that revolution had broken out in Petrograd. I must say, it is surprising that one can be so close to the center of things and yet find that everything is concealed, that one isn't informed and one learns of such momentous events almost by accident.

It was in Pskov that the Tsar abdicated on March 15, 1917. Though Father was in the same train, he was not present when Nicholas made this crucial decision. However, shortly afterwards he found himself alone with the Tsar in the dining car. They talked briefly over a glass of tea. In a matter-of-fact voice he said to Father: "Now that I am about to be freed of my responsibilities to the nation, perhaps I can fulfil my life's desire—to have a farm, somewhere in England. What do you think?"

To this seemingly casual question, Father reacted with long pent-up emotion. Only now—too late—was he being asked for his thoughts.

"What do I think?" he exclaimed. "What will become of you, of us, of Russia, now that those questionable characters are in control? Your Majesty, this is a tragic step you have taken. . . ."

Father described the response to his outburst: Nicholas remained silent. His face showed no emotion, but as he left the dining car, Father observed, he seemed hurt.

That night they returned to Mogilev, after the Tsar had signed the abdication document.

Father's diary, written at the time, describes the last days in Mogilev:

March 17 [1917, Mogilev] . . . Toward evening the train bearing the
[Dowager] Empress Maria Feodorovna who had come to say good-
bye to her son, arrived from Kiev. . . .

March 18, Sunday, Mogilev. In the morning the Tsar as usual
attended mass at the cathedral, which was jammed with
people. . . . Many cried. . . . The Tsar complained that General Alekseyev did not report anything to him any more. He spent nearly the
entire day with Maria Feodorovna.

This, no doubt, was the occasion on which Nicholas told her,
"Even Grabbe has turned against me." Years later Father was
saddened to learn of the comment.

March 19, Monday. The Tsar sorted out his personal effects and,
after lunch, went to the building that housed the General Staff, where
all officers and men [who worked there] had been assembled. In a
touching speech he thanked all for their service and said good-bye to
each one individually. The meeting left a painful impression.

March 20, Tuesday. The deputies of the provisional government,
[A. A.] Bublikov and [N. V.] Nekrasov arrived during the evening.

The former Tsar had been in Mogilev five days when a dele-
gation headed by A. A. Bublikov, sent by the Provisional
Government, arrived to take him to Tsarskoye Selo. It was
not until then that General Alekseyev, Chief of Staff was told
that the Provisional Government had decided to put Nicholas
under arrest. Almost immediately they started back, taking
with them the former Tsar together with a company of ten
soldiers placed under their orders by General Alekseyev.

In his memoirs Father says that General Alekseyev "was
undoubtedly leftist in his views," and since "he still had
complete authority to command and to direct reliable troops,"
he bears a share of the responsibility for the course of events.
He adds that Alekseyev "quickly perceived all the falsity of
his politics . . . but it was already too late."

Of Nicholas's last day in Mogilev Father says:

March 21, Wednesday. In the morning after tea the Tsar got ready for the journey. He said good-bye to the officers and men of the *Konvoy* and thanked them for their services. Then he joined Maria Feodorovna, where he waited for the time of departure. He would be accompanied on the journey by Bublikov and Nekrasov, who made all the arrangements and indicated who would be allowed to go along.

Here are further relevant comments from Father's memoirs:

Maria Feodorovna's train stood nearby and one cannot [calmly] recall that terrible moment when the Tsar, having said good-bye forever to his mother, crossed over to the train that was waiting for him. There he found himself at the complete disposal of the [provisional government's] deputies, who admitted [to the train] only [Prince Vassily] Dolgoruky, [K. A.] Naryskin, and the duty officer, *Fligel Adjutant* Duke N. N. Leuchtenberg. . . .

On March 21st the Tsar signed his last order to the troops in which, among other things, he asked the troops to obey the provisional government. This order was not given to the troops by General Alekseyev in accordance with instructions from Guchkov. . . .

. . . The [military] representatives of the Allied Powers who were at general headquarters wanted to accompany the Tsar's train [to Tsarskoye Selo] to insure his safety, but General Alekseyev declared to General Williams that there was no necessity to do so since the train would reach its destination safely. . . .

. . . The news that some representatives of the new government had come to fetch the Tsar was concealed. That is, it was not known that from that moment on, the Tsar found himself under arrest and lost his liberty. All instructions now came from the deputies who had arrived. . . .

. . . Only after the Tsar's departure from Mogilev did it become known that the provisional government had arrested him. Such a base decision of the provisional government could be carried out only because of the secretiveness surrounding the government's plans. But if knowledge of this [intent] had come earlier in Mogilev—neither those in charge [of the military establishment], nor the garrison, nor the inhabitants of the town would have so easily let the Tsar go. One can assume that General Alekseyev, the Chief of Staff, knowing about the orders of the provisional government, was already beginning to have second thoughts about his false orientation.

The oath of allegiance to the provisional government was taken only the day after the Tsar left [Mogilev], but if the directive of the provisional government regarding the arrest had become known not at the moment of the train's departure, but even an hour earlier, then, despite the Tsar's words of farewell in which he asked [the troops] to "serve the provisional government," etc., one can be entirely certain that the Tsar's order asking the troops to give loyalty to the provisional government would not have been carried out and they would have acted differently. . . .

Many people thought that Father should have gone with Nicholas when the former Emperor was taken from Mogilev. They questioned his loyalty, perhaps unaware that he was not allowed to go. For the rest of his life this accusation caused him pain.

Afterwards Father told us, "I could have made a big stir, forced my way into the train past the guards, and allowed myself to be carried out of the train by force. Everybody would have said, 'How admirable! How loyal he is! What devotion!' But I already knew that I had been excluded from the Tsar's entourage, and I just couldn't make this futile gesture. Playing to the gallery at this historic moment? No, I could not."

As I recall Father's wistful tone, I wonder whether he wasn't sorry later that he hadn't done just that. Its now known that the representatives of the Provisional Government deliberately kept the arrest secret until the last moment, telling only General Alekseyev. And it was certainly not by accident that Father was excluded from the train. He was the only one in the entire entourage who had a military force at his command. For all they knew he could have had a contingent of the Konvoy outside the station waiting to rescue Nicholas.

The day after Nicholas was taken away, Father presented himself to General Alekseyev and asked him to authorize his retirement or permit him to take a leave of absence. The General at first refused, saying, "You have now come under my command." He must have relented, however, for the next day Father arranged a leave to return to Petrograd. There he immediately tendered his resignation to the Ministry of War and was retired from the Army.

In the years to come Father found himself still pursued by the allegation that he had been remiss in his loyalty to the Tsar. The former ruler's comment to his mother—"Even Grabbe has turned against me"—suggested to her and, hence, gave currency to the idea that Father had deserted him. Maria Feodorovna had no way of knowing the context of the comment. Her son probably had in mind Father's criticism in the dining car the day he abdicated.

And all the time Father kept his pain and disappointment to himself. That, too, I did not see.

A few months before his death, we had a blow-up. It started with a minor disagreement as those things do. And then I reproached him for having failed me as a father. He was moved to say he did the best he could. We left it at that. Yet somehow this exchange brought us closer.

Father is gone. He has been dead for many years. But if there were any way for me to reach him now, I would say, "I'm sorry. Sorry that I was so blind and so unfeeling." I wish I could have told him while he was alive.

In a way I did tell him. In New York, when he was eighty-two, he became gravely ill. It was apparent he would die. Our apartments was only blocks away. I had been with him that afternoon. In the evening, Mother telephoned to say he wanted to see me.

He would not die until I got there. Then, with words that conveyed so much more than they said, he asked me to settle him more comfortably in bed. I found him very heavy. He looked at me, and in that moment we knew we forgave each other for whatever hurt we had done. I was still holding him when he gave a sigh and quietly died.

14

THE REVOLUTION COMES

Three days before the Tsar abdicated, a group of us stood in front of our living room window and looked out. At the time, the family was living in the *Konvoy* barracks, on the Neva, only a few blocks from the Liteiny Bridge. The situation at the Capital, we all knew, had become increasingly tense.

Nils and I were on Mother's left. On her right was Cossack Captain Makoukho, in command of the Petrograd contingent of the *Konvoy*. Mother was leaning slightly forward to get a better view. The captain, a big man, stood erect. He seemed more than ever imperturbable, his Oriental eyes fixed on the bridge. He gripped the back of a chair. Several regimental officers stood nearby. We were all watching the bridge.

Below us, the frozen river shone in the sunlight. Fresh snow had fallen on its icy surface during the night, and the Neva looked dazzlingly white and empty, like a frozen plain in some winter landscape. It was very cold outside that Monday morning, March 12, 1917.

"Have you had any word from Aleksander Nikolayevich?" Captain Makoukho inquired of Mother.

"Not since last Wednesday," Mother answered. "He must still be at General Headquarters with the Tsar."

We were looking in the direction of the Liteiny Bridge. On its farther side, something quite out of the ordinary was happening. Halfway across the bridge, we could see that a barricade had just been set up. On our side of the bridge stood soldiers with fixed bayonets; on the other, a large crowd approaching the bridge heaved and surged. People shouted and waved banners. Soon they were pressing against the barricade.

"Will the barricade hold?" someone asked.

"The police had better stop this disturbance before it gets out of hand," someone else remarked.

As we stood peering anxiously at the bridge, the crowd continued to push forward. For a moment we thought it would be contained. On our side of the river, a tank moved up to the bridge; then, in quick succession, two armored vehicles and more soldiers appeared. A detachment of mounted police rode briskly by under our windows. Minutes passed.

Suddenly, as we watched, the crowd broke through the barricade. A great mass of humanity swarmed over the bridge. It seemed to engulf the soldiers, the tank, the police, everything.

"Look! Look at that!" gasped Nils to me, almost in a whisper.

A Cossack lieutenant entered the room at that moment with a message for Captain Makoukho. He looked grim. "Units of the Volynsky Regiment have mutinied," he reported. "They've rushed out of their barracks, leaving their officers. A message just came through that they have joined the revolutionary crowds. . . ." He seemed incredulous.

I knew the young officer well. I had nicknamed him

Shamyl. We used to play tennis together summer evenings at
Peterhof. He had a powerful serve and beat me regularly.
Playing with him was fun, and it improved my game. He was
tall and blond and exuberant. Now he looked strained and his
uniform was not quite as neat as usual. "The revolutionaries
have invaded the Detention Prison there, on the opposite
bank," he managed to get out, trying to be calm. "They've
opened the cells, let the prisoners out. Stores are being broken into and looted. . ."

As we listened to his words, we kept our eyes on the scene
below. By now the crowd was surging past our window along
the quay.

"Let's go to my room," Nils said to me. "We'll have a better view." I followed him, and we stationed ourselves near
one of his windows.

On the quay below, a dense crowd continued to move past
our building—soldiers and sailors waving red flags and bran-
dishing guns; university and gymnasium students in their
school uniforms, many wearing red armbands; nondescript
civilians, clerks, and workers; and, here and there, prison in-
mates, still wearing their prison clothes.

"Suppose some of them take a potshot at us," I said to
Nils.

He scoffed at the idea. "Why should they bother? They
have bigger things on their minds."

"Where can they be going?"

"To the Duma, no doubt," Nils said.

The Duma, Imperial Russia's legislative assembly, had become of late the scene of violent criticism of the regime. It
held its sessions in the Tauride Palace, a short distance from
the barracks, and it turned out to be the focal point of the
Revolution.

Despite what Nils had said, I cautiously lowered myself to
the floor. My back to the window, I held up a hand mirror

and tried to use it as a periscope. It didn't work very well. Soon I got up again. My interest in the crowd was beginning to lag. I felt like an onlooker at a parade and had only a vague idea of the whys and wherefores of the uprising. Its implications escaped me. In any case, I did not think it concerned me very much. What did concern me was that my holiday from school would probably be extended. I was happy about that.

For the past several days Mother had kept me out of school. The streets were unsafe, she said. This was true enough. Excited, unruly crowds filled the center of town. They paraded with signs which read "Down with the war! We want bread!" and the police were barely able to keep the demonstrations within bounds.

As I later learned, food shortages had developed. Flour had become scarce in the capital. There was a run on the bakeries. People were going hungry, and in their hunger they became angry. In our home, thanks to Danila's foresight, our menu remained unchanged. He brought us reports that there were long lines of resentful men and women queued up in the bitter cold waiting for bread. He also said that many workers were on strike, that revolutionary songs could be heard on the streets. He shook his head. It was clear from what he said that feeling was running high not only against the Tsar, but against anyone who appeared to be well dressed.

Other serious incidents had already occurred. On the previous afternoon, when Nils had gone to the main library on the Nevsky Prospect, he had seen troops fire on a crowd that refused to disperse. Within seconds, he said, the street was empty of people except for those lying dead or wounded. Many had been passersby like Nils. Soon after Nils got home, a friend of his telephoned to say he'd heard that Georgi Vuich, a boy two grades ahead of me at the Corps, had been set upon by rioters and thrown into the canal. He drowned before anyone could come to his aid.

"The uniform is what did it," Nils remarked. "That Corps uniform spells privilege."

Apparently the school authorities agreed and decided that something had to be done to tone down the uniform. A week later we were all told to remove the Tsar's gold monogram—NII—from our epaulets. I avoided doing so as long as possible, not because of any special loyalty to the Tsar, but for aesthetic reasons. Perhaps I might add that many of the other boys so identified themselves with the monarchy that removing the epaulets seemed to them a betrayal.

The telephone rang throughout the day. Friends of the family kept calling with conflicting reports. Some said that troops loyal to the Tsar were about to quell the rebellion. Others were full of gloom. The Tsar, they feared, would abdicate and plunge the country into chaos.

The sun went down, and night came. Then around eight o'clock that evening we heard insistent pounding on our front door. When Yegor opened it, several disheveled soldiers pushed their way in. With them were two young sailors whose navy caps were angled cockily on their heads. "*Obysk!*" their leader announced as they entered—"A search!" He was a big man with a livid scar on his neck. Two clips of machine gun bullets made an X on his chest. "Do you have any arms?" he demanded. Without waiting for an answer, the intruders trooped through our living room. They cast curious glances at the furnishings. Mother, Nils, and Yegor followed them into Father's study. I trailed behind, fearful all the while lest the soldiers' menacing manner lead to violence. "Aha! Arms!" exclaimed a young soldier, lifting an ancient pistol from a display of antique arms on the wall. "Put that back!" the leader commanded. "Go on, put it back! It's no use to us."

The soldiers and sailors stood around uncertainly for a few moments. Then, following their leader, they left.

"What are we coming to?" lamented Yegor as he closed the front door after them. "How do they dare? . . ."

Only minutes after the soldiers had ranged through our home, their search of the apartment upstairs was apparently resisted. We heard a shot and wondered what had happened. Captain Makoukho reassured us: one of the soldiers had fired his gun at random. We might have been less lucky. As we learned later, an acquaintance of Father, General G. E. Stackelberg who lived on Millionnaya Street, was shot during just such a search as ours.

The first day of the Revolution finally came to an end.

The next day Captain Makoukho stopped by. He told us that the upheaval had been relatively bloodless and confined almost exclusively to the capital. The rest of the country had not yet taken any part in the uprising and knew next to nothing of what was happening in Petrograd. The probable reason we had not heard from Father, he said, was that the Tsar had left General Headquarters at Mogilev, bound for Tsarskoye Selo, and Father was doubtless with him in the Imperial train. That was the time the train was diverted to Pskov.

The Tsar had given no indication that he might abdicate, the Captain had heard, but already a new government was taking shape at the Capital.

A Soviet of Workers Deputies had also come into existence. These two bodies, competing for power, were meeting in the same building, the Tauride Palace. Captain Makoukho sounded discouraged as he gave us the news.

On the third day after the Revolution had begun, Nils and I ventured out of the house to reconnoiter. Outside, everything seemed peaceful, but when we reached the Liteiny Prospect we were immediately struck by the emptiness of this usually busy thoroughfare. All shops were closed; streetcars were not running; there were few pedestrians, and no traffic. Only military cars, manned by soldiers and armed civilians, dashed about. A block further on we came upon the still smoldering burned-out ruins of the Circuit Court. We looked for a newspaper but could find none. On our way home along a side street we saw what looked like a pile of logs; it turned out to be the bodies of dead policemen, stacked like firewood and partly covered with snow.

"Ugh!" I said, turning away.

"The crowd took it out on the police," Nils said. We hurried on in silence.

"I must find out what's going on at the Tauride Palace," Nils said as we neared home. "That seems to be where things are happening." We parted at our doorstep, and he went on.

I found Mother home. She, too, had gone for a short walk, and I could see at once that something had upset her.

"Imagine!" she said to me. "I just ran into Countess Sheremetiev; and how do you suppose she greeted me? She said: 'Isn't it wonderful?' and I said, 'What's wonderful?' and she said, 'Why, the Revolution, of course!' and I said, 'Well, Countess, you're hardly the one to rejoice. It is precisely people like us who stand to lose everything.' "

Mother was still angry, but I wasn't paying much attention. I was too full of what I had seen on the street. Later, when I repeated to Nils Countess Sheremetiev's comment, he said, "That's not surprising. Everybody knows she has leftist views."

I was beginning to realize that the Revolution meant something different to each person. While Countess Sheremetiev saw it as progress toward a better society, Mother could see in it only ominous signs for the future. To me it was a welcome holiday from school. But to Matvei, my valet, the Revolution seemed to hold the promise of a better day. He planned to open a shoemaker's shop.

15

THE OTHER SEX

A week after the outbreak of the Revolution my school reopened. But what a different place it was! Rules and regulations were no longer enforced. Discipline had broken down. Nobody could concentrate on his studies. There was a mood of rebellion everywhere. We all wanted to throw off restraint. Opportunity soon presented itself. The irony was that the sons of the most privileged should want to have a revolution of their own.

With the reopening of the Corps it was announced by Deputy Director General Rittikh—some of the boys said he was wearing a red armband—that we would all be detained at the school overnight. Why? we asked. To take part, Colonel Zarzhevsky explained, in an official service in the school's chapel. It was to be in memory of the "victims of the Revolution." We all knew that our schoolmate, Georgi Vuich, had been one of the victims. We also knew the Government meant the workers and soldiers killed in the upheaval. It was clear to us that this was a political gesture. Nobody actually could be certain who among those being buried with great fanfare in the public square were the victims and who were not. The Provisional Government evidently thought it expedient to proclaim a holiday and order a national memorial service. No doubt the school authorities feared that poor attendance by the Corps would be interpreted as lack of support for the Revolution.

At first we were all furious at being detained, but not for long. Our anger disappeared when one of the boys suggested that we use the occasion to have a celebration that night in the dormitory. A splendid idea, we all agreed. To make the party really festive, a group of us went out on the Nevsky Prospect with the intention of buying wine and possibly bringing back some women. Big occasions inspire big ideas. Needless to say, our project was in complete violation of school regulations.

It was not the school authorities, however, who put a damper on our festivities; it was our youth. We were still too young to know how adults go about raising hell. So we just sat around the dormitory drinking wine and eating chicken sandwiches bought at the neighborhood store—a very tame affair.

When I got home the next day, frustrated in my fantasies, I decided that I would go out and really raise hell—this time on my own. I had just turned fifteen. Up until then, I had not been allowed to go out by myself after dark. So I felt extremely daring when I left the house around nine in the evening, unescorted, and headed uptown. My intention was to get a taste of the capital's night life, perhaps even pick up a girl. Alas, I did not know how to find the night spots, and though I tried to look self-assured as I strode along the Nevsky and passed many women—some of whom smiled at me—I was too shy to approach any of them. I wound up in a cabaret, alone.

As I settled into my seat in the darkened house, I glanced around. Nearby was a young couple holding hands. They had some liqueur glasses on a little table in front of them; I took my cue from them and ordered a liqueur. On the stage a humorous skit was in progress. It was called "Ivanov, Pavel" after the principal character in the skit, a teen-age student who coped successfully with stupid school authorities. I had heard that audiences identified the school authorities with the Imperial government and that the veiled allusions sprinkled through the skit accounted for its popularity. I was not too interested in the political gibes. What I did enjoy was the music. Tuneful and rousing, it consisted of catchy operetta melodies skillfully strung together.

After I left the cabaret, I did not know what to do next. Besides, I had no money left. So I went home with a rather letdown feeling.

Looking back, I have a sneaking admiration for my fifteen-year-old self. At least I tried.

As soon as Father had tendered his resignation to the Ministry of War, he started proceedings to have the *Konvoy* sent to the Caucasus and there reassigned as a group. His argument—that the *Konvoy* was closely identified with the Tsar—proved persuasive. The Provisional Government was pleased to see it go. Father arranged to have all *Konvoy* contingents that were stationed in or near the capital—perhaps three hundred men with families, horses, and personal belongings—entrain at the capital and at Tsarskoye Selo and return home. This was not easily accomplished in a time of internal crisis and with a war on, and Father was proud to have done it and taken care of his men.

Before the *Konvoy* left for the Caucasus, its officers gave a farewell party for Father in our barracks apartment. In memory of their service together, they presented Father with a small silver chalice from Fabergé inscribed with the signatures of all the officers. This elegant little drinking cup now rests on the mantlepiece of our Cape Cod home. I get a special thrill out of tracing with my eye the signatures of Captain Makoukho and of the young lieutenant, who first brought us the news of the Revolution nearly sixty years ago.

The officers' party had curious repercussions for me. It so happened that my valet Matvei, an unexpectedly resourceful man, saw a way of turning this event to our mutual advantage. The morning after the party, he woke me up as usual at seven. Then he lighted the stove and hung my clothes in front of the fire. As was his custom, he held my bathrobe as he urged me to get out of bed. After a while I sat up, and as I did so, he promptly pulled on my stockings and handed me my clothes. While I was dressing, he usually regaled me with stories of village life or of his latest adventures in the city. These tales always concerned women, and he made clear to me that women liked him.

He was tall, muscular, and broad-shouldered, about thirty years old—a citified peasant who had lived long enough at the Capital to learn its ways. Garrulous and sometimes insolent, he had a strong element of the rogue in him. Withal, he was good-natured—a good sort—and I enjoyed hearing him boast about his conquests. He took such relish in his stories.

"Would you believe it?" he'd say. "On Sunday—I guess it was a week ago—in church I met a girl from my home province, from Tambov. . . . A pretty thing she was, solidly built and ample where it matters. Well, as we left the church and walked along the avenue, chatting sort of friendly-like, she suddenly stopped. 'Here we are,' she said, pointing to a house across the street. 'It's where I live.'

"You won't believe me, but it's the honest truth! She took me up the back stairs of her master's apartment—they were away somewhere—settled me in their pantry and treated me to wine and cheese and freshly salted cucumbers. They were delicious. . . ."

He paused to rub his knee and savor these pleasurable memories.

"Well, let me tell you," he went on. "You just don't stand on ceremony in a case like that. Don't hesitate. Get 'er legs up and go to it." He paused again reflectively. "What a girl. . . ."

Fascinated, I listened while Matvei talked and strutted.

On the morning after the *Konvoy* officers' party, Matvei couldn't wait to tell me that a lot of liquor had been left in Father's part of the apartment and nobody had as yet cleared away the debris. There were quite a few bottles of vodka and cognac left half-empty, he reported. And, as he handed me my shirt, he looked at me sideways, saying, "I could get you a tidy sum for what's left in those bottles."

I stopped buttoning my shirt. "What's that you say?"

"Well . . . when your father's orderly cleans up later this morning, he'll take the vodka and he'll take the cognac from the half-empty bottles, and he'll sell it. Sure enough, that's what he'll do! He'll get fifty rubles for the vodka, I reckon, and another fifty for the cognac. So why let him have it when I can sell it for you just as easily with a 10 percent commission? That would leave you at least ninety rubles. You'd certainly have plenty of use for that!"

"I guess so," I said uncertainly.

"I mean it's about time you had some experience . . ."

"What do you mean?"

"Well, experience . . . that is, I mean women. and I can arrange it for you."

"Yes, yes, of course."

I was embarrassed and wanted to break off the conversation. Sex was never mentioned in our family, at least not in my presence. There were few even oblique references to it among the adults. Once at dinner I heard Uncle Kolya make a joke about woman as a receptacle—it was a play on words. I did not know what he was talking about and wouldn't have noticed anything except that Mother hushed him up.

Another time, Uncle Kolya told a story about Uncle Sasha, apparently unaware that I was around. It seems Uncle Sasha was asked if there was any difference among prostitutes in different parts of the world. He answered, "I don't know, really. Too much bother, you know. Getting undressed, and then, well, you have to get dressed again. . . ." At that point everybody laughed and I wondered what was so funny.

I also remember a visit to the bathroom. I must have been eight at the time. I confided to Koukoulya that nothing could possibly be more pleasurable. But he replied, "You're mistaken there. Something else is better!" When I asked what it was, he answered, "You just wait. You'll find out soon enough," and refused to say more.

Koukoulya's response was typical. In our house everyone was tight-lipped on the subject of sex. I did not learn anything about the relationship between men and women or even where babies come from until I entered the cadet school. Then a flood of information and misinformation poured in on me. At home, only Matvei talked to me freely.

"You're fifteen now," he went on, "—not a kid any more—and I can arrange it for you. I know a nice little woman here in town. She's just right for you. You can stay a couple of hours if you want to, and it will cost you only ten rubles—a bargain these days, with prices rising all the time. You don't want to be like your brother Nils, do you?"

"Why, what's the matter with Nils?"

"Just that he's afraid of women. That's what's the matter. If you ask me, I don't believe he's had anything to do with women yet. And he's nineteen already."

"How do you know he hasn't?"

"How can I help knowing? Time and again I've tried to get him interested, but he won't make a move. Afraid, that's what he is. He won't even talk about it."

"Really?"

"And you don't want to be like him, do you?"

"Well . . ."

"Let me arrange it for you, a meeting with this wench."

"I have no money."

"Oh, but you have! You just go into your father's study while everyone's asleep. Empty the open bottles into a couple of buckets. I'll get them for you. Make sure you leave some in each bottle so it won't look suspicious. Then turn the buckets over to me, and I'll do the rest." Though tempted, I still wavered. "It's your father's orderly or you. How about it?"

Armed with two buckets, though still hesitant, I tiptoed into Father's study. Disorder everywhere—bottles, cigarette ashes, dirty plates—as if the occupants had suddenly picked themselves up and gone off. Everything was quiet except the pounding of my heart. I moved around the room, picking up bottles and emptying them as fast as I could. Then, with the vodka bucket in one hand and the cognac bucket in the other, I was soon back in my room, where Matvei was waiting. He cast a quick approving look at the contents of the buckets.

"A good haul," he said. "More vodka than I had expected."

The next morning Matvei brought me 100 rubles, and I counted out his 10 percent. I stuck 20 rubles in my pocket, and hid the rest under the desk blotter. Then we were ready for our expedition. We took the streetcar up the Liteiny Prospect, transferred, and got off near the railroad station. Down a side street we went, entered a poorly lit building, and walked up several flights of stairs.

"Wait here a minute," Matvei said at the landing. He knocked on a door. The door opened a crack. There was a brief consultation. Matvei came back. "I've arranged it all.

You go inside and wait," he said. "She's making it a bargain for you—because it's the first time—only ten rubles. Give the money to her before you leave. And now I'm going." He hastened down the stairs while I stood there. Well, I had come this far, and I might as well go the whole way. Screwing up my courage, I went in and closed the door behind me.

There was no one in the room. It was small and sparsely furnished. I took off my overcoat, hung it on a peg, and sat down. I felt as nervous as if I were about to have a session with the dentist. In fact, the place reminded me of a dentist's anteroom. Trying to look nonchalant, I picked up a newspaper from a table and started to read it. But I couldn't concentrate.

"Good morning," said a woman's voice. I looked up. A brunette, about thirty years old, stood on the threshold. She was quite attractive. Through her negligee I could see her ample figure and large breasts. She gave me a quick but not unfriendly look. "Nervous?" she said sympathetically. "It's going to be all right. Come this way."

The next room was even smaller. A huge bed was almost all there was.

"Well," said the brunette, "aren't you going to take off your clothes?" Awkwardly, I took off my shoes, socks, shirt.

"I see you have nothing with you, have you, to protect yourself?" I didn't know what she meant. "I guess not," I answered.

"Well, you should have. My advice to you is never to have anything to do with a strange woman without protecting yourself."

I was silent. She was silent, too. "Here, take this," she said, handing me something. "Take it, take it," she repeated as I hesitated, "and use it. Yes, use it!"

Try as I will to remember what happened next, all that comes to mind is a merry-go-round with horses going up and down. Her voice I remember very well. It was gentle and reassuring.

When I handed her a ten-ruble bank note, she smiled. "My name is Sonia," she said. "If you want to come back, I'll be glad to see you." Though I never returned, I was grateful. I've always liked the name Sonia.

I found Nils waiting for me at the door when I got home.

"Just think," he said holding me by the sleeve so that I wouldn't get away, "last night, a battery across the river had its guns trained on this house. . . . It took a lot of doing by Father's friend, Tereshchenko—he's in the new government now, you know—to keep them from blowing up the barracks. And all the while we were peacefully asleep. Imagine that!"

While Nils was talking, I was thinking: Is he really afraid of women? Matvei says so, but Matvei tends to exaggerate; and Nils would never tell me. Still, only a short time earlier, when sex came into our conversation, he made a face and said, "Disgusting." I wonder where he got that idea? He was nineteen then.

Nils was still talking. "Kerensky," he was saying, "is the man to watch. The others? Well, they can't cope. You mark my word! Kerensky is the man." Nils was wrong on Kerensky.

That night when I went to bed, I thought over the day and recalled what Matvei had said about Nils. He is my brother, I thought. Yet, what do I know about him? Brilliant and accomplished and plays the piano well, and says he is against the Revolution. That isn't very much. Do I know any more? He never talks about his feelings. He must really be a rather solitary person. None of his school friends ever visit him here. Is it because Mother once embarrassed one of them? Perhaps, but it's more likely that he prefers to be alone, playing the piano or studying a Wagner score, or maybe reading. He is always reading, even on the street, walking along twirling his cane, oblivious to people.

The strongest bond we have, I mused, is music. I like music, too, though I can't play the piano or any other instrument. Temperamentally, though, I guess we're different. Even in his music he doesn't let out his feelings; there is a certain dryness. And, come to think of it, he doesn't want to hear what I have to say on any really serious subject. When I try to tell a story even, he taps his foot on the floor. I guess I'm too slow for him. He is brainier than I am. Perhaps I bore him; for, after all, he is older than I am. Still, I was the first to get to know a woman. . . .

16

WE SEEK REFUGE

As the turmoil of the Revolution subsided and the summer of 1917 came on, Father decided that times were still too uncertain for us to bury ourselves in the country. Instead, with Grand Duke Georgi Mikhailovich, the Tsar's uncle, he rented a villa in Finland, not far from the Capital.

The Grand Duke was a tall, friendly, fiftyish man with long whiskers and a kindly smile. He had brought with him to the Rettiaervi villa his male secretary, personal valet, and an excellent cook for whom we were grateful. There was always caviar on the table, and I helped myself liberally, much to Mother's annoyance. She enjoined me to use restraint. As she put it, "Our share of the expense does not include caviar."

Talk at the dinner table reflected everyone's concern about developments in Russia. Georgi Mikhailovich was torn between his wish to be with his family, then in England, and his loyalty to Russia. He felt that it would be unseemly, even disloyal, to leave his country in a time of crisis. To allay his anxiety, he played three-handed bridge with Nils and me. Nils already knew the game, but I didn't, so Nils taught me. Ten years later these lessons helped me find a job in Los

Mother wearing pearl necklace, only valuable saved after the Revolution. (1903)

Father in field uniform as commander of Konvoy. (1915)

Author, aged thirteen, in uniform of Corps des Pages. (1915)

Grand Duchess Anastasia, the Tsar's youngest daughter, on the Imperial yacht *Standart*. (1912)

The Empress and daughters on board the
Imperial yacht with Court Minister Count
V. B. Fredericks. (1912)

The Empress with Father at Mogilev. (1916)

The Tsar relaxes near Mogilev six months before the Revolution. With him are three of his daughters and members of his retinue. Left to right: Grand Duchess Olga, Countess A. Hendrikov, lady-in-waiting, Grand Duchess Marie. Behind her, Grand Duchess Anastasia. Colonel A.A. Mordvinov, aide-de-camp, kneels behind the Tsar. At far right is the author's father taking picture with "squeeze bulb" cable release. (1916)

Princess Margaret, the British minelayer on which the Grabbe family escaped from Riga. (*Photo:* Imperial War Museum, London)

The author, age seventeen, after rescue. (1919)

The epergne presented by refugees to Captain H. H. Smyth of *Princess Margaret*.

400 refuges of all nation-
will always retain a grate-
from the bolschevik in
lant captain of H.M.S.
officers

alities, assembled in Riga
ful memory of their rescue
January 1919 by the ga-
"Princess Margaret"
and men

The Tsar looking from the window of the Imperial train. (1916)

Angeles when I was hungry and without work.

The Grand Duke, as it happened, returned to Petrograd despite his friends' entreaties. Once back in the Capital, he was arrested, imprisoned, and eventually shot. His brother, the historian, Grand Duke Nikolai Mikhailovich, was executed at the same time.

During our stay in Finland, Nils and I had our first serious quarrel. I had an invitation to visit my school friend, Count Nikolai Rebinder, who was spending the summer a few hours' journey away. To get there, I planned to board the passenger steamer on the Saimaan Canal. The canal went right past our villa. I planned to take my bicycle with me, but discovered too late that it was broken. So I decided to borrow Nils's bicycle, only I did not ask him—I was afraid he'd refuse. My intention was to take it to the canal lock, hide it, and pick it up when I boarded the boat. I was walking it along the path bordering the canal when Nils intercepted me. Without a word he jerked the bicycle away from me. I promptly wrested it back. Some blows were exchanged, and angry words spoken. The struggle ended when Nils tore from my neck my gold cross and chain. They dropped into the canal, and I fell in, too. I don't know whether he pushed me or I lost my balance. Meanwhile, Nils wheeled the bicycle back to the house. This was the first time Nils and I had fought. It was clearly my fault.

Something else I did that day also was wrong. Mother had given me a little money for the trip, but not enough, I thought. So instead of paying my fare on the boat, I climbed on board while the boat was in the canal lock. In this way I got a free ride and a free meal, but felt shamefaced all the way. Like Pinocchio disregarding the counsel of the Blue Fairy, I, too, forgot what Vladimir Aleksan'ch had tried to teach me.

When later in the summer we returned to our suburban

villa, the capital was ominously still. The Bolsheviks had tried
to stage a coup, and Lenin was in town. I followed these
events in the newspapers. But I was just fifteen and bent on
having a good time. Such matters did not concern me.

Every afternoon I played tennis with the banker's daughter,
who lived across the road. Several evenings a week I went to
the circus to watch professional wrestling, my latest enthusiasm.

Meantime, Father's friends at the Imperial Yacht Club had
been urging him to leave the Capital. His association with the
Tsar, they said, made it risky for him to stay in Petrograd:
"Why not take temporary refuge in some remote provincial
town?" At first Father was skeptical, but once convinced, he
acted quickly. He bought tickets for Sochi, a semitropical resort in the Caucasus on the Black Sea, and within a week we
were off.

Not all of us went. Nils, recently graduated from the lycée,
was at officers' training school. He would join us later.
Georges was to remain in Petrograd, looked after by our butler Yegor. Mr. Boyle had long since gone to join the British
army. "Nobody will harm Georges if he stays here," Mother
said. As it worked out, Mother was right in a way.

Before we left, Father rented our suburban villa to a candy
manufacturer. As a deposit, we received eighty pounds of
chocolate. This unusual arrangement was thought up by
Mother, who wanted to make sure that she had a supply
large enough for the entire trip. Chocolate, she knew, was
getting scarce.

And so, one evening in late August 1917, our chauffeur
Vlasyouk drove us to the railroad station, where we took a
fast train for the Caucasus. In addition to Father, Mother, and
me, our party included Mother's maid Emilia and Fedyushkin,
who had decided to continue as Father's orderly. Also with us
was our French bulldog, Bullo.

In those days Sochi was not widely known. Nor was it easy to get there. To reach it, we had to change trains, sit up all night in a slow local train, and hire a motorboat to go the last fifty miles. We were advised not to attempt this last lap of our journey by car because bandits infested the entire coastal highway.

When our motorboat reached Sochi, it docked at the Caucasian Riviera Hotel, where we planned to stay. Although the name of the hotel sounded pretentious, the group of white buildings that made up the complex was fittingly imposing. Beyond the hotel we could see a distant chain of snowcapped mountains: the main Caucasus Range. The town of Sochi itself was located some miles inland. It had a few stores, a rickety post office, a movie house.

As with most resort hotels, the Caucasian Riviera attracted a variety of people. What they all had in common was substantial bank accounts. Among them were vacationing army and naval officers, with or without their wives; widows and divorcées; merchants, lawyers, and bankers with their families. I still remember some of the more colorful guests. I think of a young matron, the wife of a Cossack officer. She was much talked about because every evening she swam a mile out to sea regardless of the weather. Impressive as was her prowess in the water, her figure, everyone agreed, was equally so.

Also staying at the hotel was a male ballet dancer who pranced about and introduced himself to everyone. He wore a different suit of clothes on every occasion. Although I started counting, I soon lost track of the number. One of his suits particularly intrigued me; its color was deep violet. I not only envied him his clothes, as I owned only one suit, I also envied him his assurance and the ease with which he waltzed at the hotel dances.

Notable, too, among the guests was a *ménage à trois*. It consisted of two men and a young woman. All three were svelte, well-groomed, and elegantly dressed. They always ate their meals together, and provided the other guests with an endless topic of conversation. There was much speculation about the woman: whether she slept with both men, taking turns, or both at the same time; or whether one of the men made love to her as well as to the other man. Some even thought she had been brought along by two homosexuals purely as a decoy.

After six months there was as yet little evidence of the Revolution in Sochi. Most of the hotel guests spent their days sunning themselves on the beach or lounging on their balconies. In bad weather, some played cards. Others congregated in the game room to play pool. Pool was a game I liked. I had learned it at Vasilievskoye. In Sochi I played as often as I could, but not as often as I wanted to because the hotel charged a rental for the tables and I never had more than a few rubles.

As I remember it, the game I played in Russia differed from the game in the United States. The pockets were narrower, admitting balls only at a right angle. Superior strategy— maneuvering the balls with every shot to a position as disadvantageous to one's opponent as possible—mattered as much as the ability to pocket balls. It is tempting to read here a difference in cultural conditioning. Perhaps Americans, responding to their mobile and changeable environment, are loath to postpone action and aim at quick results, whereas Russians don't mind waiting for the right opportunity before they act.

But to return to Sochi. Among the guests at the hotel was a rich Moscow merchant, Safonov, who was vacationing with his wife and family: a daughter, Nadya, nineteen; and a son, Seryozha, seventeen. Though not too bright, Nadya was very pretty, so pretty that I soon fancied myself in love with her. But Nadya scorned me. She had her eye on a young naval officer. I came to know her through her brother, Seryozha. He and I met at the pool table.

Seryozha was a typical son of a rich merchant. I guess that's the reason he was well supplied with money. When we played pool together, he usually paid for the rental of the table. He also treated me to chocolate bars, the price of which was astronomical. I relished his largess because Mother was niggardly—she had special tongs for cutting her chocolate into very small pieces.

Seryozha fascinated me. I had never known anyone like him before. He was tall and blue-eyed, and he seemed older than his years. He parted his hair in the middle rather too carefully, and his clothes were rather too expensive. He wore sports shirts open at the neck. His manner was carefree and impudent, and, as I soon discovered, he was not only cynical; he was totally amoral. Watching the easy way he had with older women, I half believed the stories he told of his conquests.

Once when we were sitting on the jetty in front of the hotel, Seryozha said, "Tell me, how do you view women?" The question was unexpected. I wasn't sure what he was driving at.

"Women?" I asked nonplussed.

"I mean do you look on women primarily as persons or as females?"

"Well," I said, trying to gain time, "it all depends . . ."

He didn't wait for an answer. "I look on women as females," he said emphatically. "They know it, too—and like it. Women want to feel they are attractive and desirable. I tell them so. It sure pays off." He paused. "There are so many women in this hotel, alone, without a man! Why, I could have a different one every night."

I knew he was boasting. Still, if I encouraged him to talk, I might learn something. The world of women was a mystery to me. I felt tongue-tied and awkward in the company of pretty girls. "Go on," I urged.

"Well, in regard to women, I find you need a system. Without a system you're lost. It takes planning and scouting around. . . ."

"Did you say scouting?"

"I did. Well, take this place, for instance, this hotel. I started out by buttering up that blonde who handles reservations—bought her some candy, made her some compliments about her hair, and all that sort of thing. Softened her up, in other words, until she let me see the hotel register."

"What good is that?"

"Why, it's essential. The register gave me the names and room numbers of all the women staying here. I copied them off—all those who might be divorced, widowed, or without their husbands. Then I started my investigation on the third floor of the main building. I watched the women come and go, waited for each one to leave her room. This way I picked out the ones I liked best, eliminating those with children, aunts, or other relatives around. That narrowed down the possibilities."

I was incredulous. In my amazement I could only say, "Go on, go on."

"Well, having spotted some one woman who appealed to me particularly, and knowing that she was all alone there in her room, I'd wait for her to come back from the beach, and knock on the door. When she opened it, I'd look embarrassed and say my sister had asked me to meet her here. I'd introduce myself and start a conversation. I'd look surprised because my sister wasn't there and say that I was sure she must be on her way. 'May I wait for her a second?' I'd ask. And by that time I'd be inside the door, and I'd sit down and pay my hostess some compliment, like, 'You certainly have beautiful eyes!' A little obvious, but never mind. When it comes to compliments, women aren't critical. That's one of their weak points. They drink it in, whatever you hand out." He stopped to ponder this deep truth.

"Now note that all the time, while I'd be taking these pre-liminary steps, I'd know she was without a man. To know this, I assure you, is a great advantage. Invaluable, in fact.

"What next, you probably wonder? Well, now was the time to play my second trump. In case you don't know it, women don't like to be dragged off to bed right off the bat. A little romancing is necessary—to get things going. So I'd get up and walk over to the window and sigh and tell her I had never met anyone quite so attractive—just like a beautiful rose. In fact, I'd say, I'd like to bring her some roses if she'd permit it. She'd laugh and say, 'You're a funny one,' or some-thing like that. Then I'd say, 'I see my sister isn't coming after all,' and I'd get up and leave. The groundwork would be laid."

"What then?" I asked.

"Well, what do you suppose? I'd wait a day or two and then go back, take her some roses." There was a silence, and then Seryozha said, "Why don't you try it? The method is foolproof . . . well, almost . . ." There was another silence, then he added, "Of course you have to have a little capital. Not much, but something you can invest—like any other enterprise—so you can buy some candy and some flowers, and all that sort of thing, at the right moment. Why don't you try it?" he repeated. "It works like magic."

"I have no money," I said dejectedly.

"What of it? Get hold of some."

"It's not so easy. Where?"

Seryozha raised his eyebrows, and his face tightened. He looked like a hunting dog on a hot spoor. "There you go," he said, putting his arm reassuringly on my shoulder. "First I gather you have no woman, and now you tell me you have no money. Why not?" He waited, then went on, "It's all the same, no matter what you're after, just like any other enterprise. Things don't drop into your lap; you have to do something."

"Do what?"

"Well, in your case, get hold of money; persuade your parents to give you some."

"They say they don't have any."

"Nonsense! It's just a way to hold you off. I saw your father paying the hotel clerk. His wallet was bulging with thousand-ruble bills . . . while you're so broke you cannot even rent a pool table for an hour. Your father wouldn't even feel it if you relieved him of a few thousand—persuaded him to part with it."

"But how?"

Seryozha did not answer. He just walked away, and I concluded that he was only talking. A week later, however, I again came upon him sitting on the jetty. "I think I've solved your problem," he announced, looking mysterious.

"Problem?"

"I've found a way for you to get some money from your parents."

"You have? How?"

"Simple. Kidnap yourself and ask for a small ransom."

"Fantastic!"

"Not in the least. It can be done—quite easily in fact." Here was the merchant making his sales pitch. "There was a kidnapping in the next town last month. Do you remember? You must have read about it in the paper. So why not a kidnapping in this town? Anyhow, I have looked into it, arranged it all. . . ."

Seryozha always amazed me. All the things he could think up! He was remarkable in this respect. And now he paused for a moment, then went on: "There are a couple of musicians, a pianist and a violinist, who play at the movie house in town. They share an apartment, and they're friends of mine. I have talked over your problem with them. In fact, I arranged to take you there some evening. They agreed to put you up—for a small fee, of course. You and I can dream up a note to your father saying that you'll be released as soon as he delivers 5000 rubles to some tree stump. Meantime, you stay in hiding and I'll keep you posted. Then we'll collect the money: 1000 each for the musicians, 1000 for me, and 2000 for you. Ah! Think of it. All that's required is a little daring on your part."

"It's too impractical," I said.

I thought that if I put the matter in these terms, Seryozha would desist. But he wasn't easily discouraged. He thought a minute, then he said, "Maybe you think your father loves his money more than he loves you? Maybe you are afraid to put him to the test?"

"I'm not afraid," I said. "Let's go ahead."

Two days later, after dark, Seryozha led me up a flight of stairs in a back street behind the movie house. The two musicians lived in a small apartment over a garage.

When we entered, Seryozha introduced me and we sat down at once around the kitchen table. We had soon composed a note to Father that the pianist printed in red ink. He signed it in bold capital letters: THE MARK OF THE RED HOOF.

The next few days I spent in the musicians' apartment. I did not like either of them. The pianist was a short fellow with a big scar across his face. The violinist, a bigger man with ruddy cheeks and oversized ears, had a hearty manner that was insincere. I must admit I was beginning to have second thoughts. I felt uneasy about the whole enterprise.

On the third day, Seryozha came by, and announced that Father had done nothing.

"Nothing?"

"Nothing at all," Seryozha said looking aggrieved. He then reported that there had been some vague rumors about me at the hotel, but it appeared that Father had not told anybody that I had disappeared, not even the police. This raised a problem. If Father ignored the note, I asked Seryozha, and did not leave the money in the tree trunk as directed, what happened next? Seryozha didn't know. He was extremely breezy about it all and soon departed, saying he would be back sometime that evening. "We have to hold a council of war," he said as he was leaving, "decide on the next step."

I stood at the window watching Seryozha walk away; and as he turned the corner and disappeared from view, I suddenly felt free—rid of his influence and of the hold he had on me. I realized that I had been a fool, a clumsy and dishonest one at that. I guessed what Father must be thinking: that I was trying to play a nasty prank on him. And he was right. I felt mortified and exasperated with myself. My feeling of humiliation brought back the words of my tutor. Any wrong you do to others hurts you, too, he'd said. I knew now what Vladimir Aleksan'ch had meant. And I was ready to make amends: If I could, I wanted to retrieve the situation. To admit publicly what I had tried to do would be intolerable. Being lowered in my own eyes was bad enough. I must somehow contrive to reappear at the hotel without embarrassment to anyone, my parents or myself. But how? Was there a way? I thought about it all afternoon.

When Seryozha and the two musicians came that evening and we sat down to plan the next move, I had my mind made up. I told them what I had to do. I added that I was counting on their cooperation. Words like *police* and *implicated* helped to persuade them that what I proposed was in their interest as well as mine.

So it happened that after midnight the two musicians and I left the apartment and started out on a long walk to the seashore. Our destination was a bench on a lonely path which ran along the beach. As I had anticipated, no one was around at that hour. Following my plan, I sat down on the bench and the musicians tied me to it with a piece of rope they had brought for the purpose. I felt the rope around my ankles and my wrists. It seemed secure. Still, I wanted it tightened, and I asked the musicians to put a handkerchief in my mouth and use a cord to hold the handkerchief in place. When all of this was done, the two musicians paused uncertainly and one of them said, "Hope you're all right." With that they turned and left, hurrying down the path without a backward glance.

And then I was alone, facing myself—a damaged image of myself. I knew that sitting there all night without an overcoat, tied to the bench and gagged, would be painful. October nights in Sochi could be chilly. But that's the way it had to be, painful or not. My family would look to me for a face-saving device, and this had to be it. I probably would have several hours ahead of me before anyone came along to rescue me.

I sat there waiting, grimly patient. Before me the sea looked motionless and black. There was no moon. The waves lapped on the beach. Occasionally a seagull screeched, but otherwise there was no sound. One hour passed, and then another. A fresh breeze sprang up. It gradually penetrated my clothes, chilling me. The rope bit into my skin. It hurt. I cursed myself. What had possessed me, anyhow? The money? A veiled, unconscious wish to show up my parents? Perhaps some impulse I did not even understand? If anyone was to accept my story that the kidnappers abandoned me at this lonely spot, I

would have to be knocked out when I was found—incoherent
enough to lead people's thoughts away from the idea that I
had engineered the thing myself.

Sometime before dawn a man approached. He lurched
along, unsteady on his feet. He must have been on his way
home from a drinking bout. As he drew near, I started making noises to attract his attention. Finally he saw me and
stopped abruptly. He took one look, then veered away.
Perhaps he thought he was seeing things.

Another hour passed. In the sky I noticed the first light of
dawn. My legs began to hurt. Maybe the rope was interfering
with my circulation. The light increased, and then a man and
a woman came walking briskly in my direction. I guessed
they were hotel employees en route to their jobs. As they
came by, the woman stopped. "Look at that!" she exclaimed,
grabbing the man by the sleeve and pointing at me. I made
more noises in my throat. This time, I thought, I'll be freed.
But I was wrong. Instead of untying me, they held a whis-
pered consultation and hurried on.

Again I was alone. By then, I was quite numb and desper-
ately cold. I comforted myself with the thought that someone
was bound to come along. And so they did—two detectives in
a car. Apparently the couple had gone to the police. The detectives untied me and took me to the police station. Someone
telephoned Father. I was given a cup of coffee.

Father soon came in a taxi and took me home. He was silent. As we drove up to the hotel, he turned to me and said,
"We had a letter from Prince Oldenburg, who is somewhere
up north, inviting us to stay in one of the apartments in his
palace in Gagry, south of here. We've decided to move there.
Nils has arrived from Petrograd. He and Mother have gone
ahead. The car for Gagry will pick us up at noon. It's a couple
of hours' drive. So now you try to get some sleep until I
waken you." He didn't scold me, recriminate, ask for details.

In fact, for years none of my family ever spoke to me of the kidnapping, never alluded to it in any way. And yet, their silence left the matter unresolved.

In time I was reminded of the incident. Father's jealous brother, Uncle Misha, hadn't been able to resist an opportunity to taunt him. "It's perfectly obvious," he snapped, "that he kidnapped himself." Father never told me what Uncle Misha had said. Mother did.

17

GAGRY IS A TRAP

When we settled down in Prince Oldenburg's palace in Gagry, everything was peaceful. "An ideal spot in which to sit out the Revolution," Father remarked. It was then mid-November 1917.

Prince Aleksander Petrovich Oldenburg, older relative of the Tsar, was Gagry's founder. Exploring the Black Sea coast he had been charmed by the wildness of the place: a village nestled on a narrow coastal strip; towering mountains and sea; palms and a balmy climate. As he told Father, he had been so impressed he decided to turn Gagry into a Russian Cannes. Accordingly, he built a large hotel at the base of the tallest mountain, and up the road a bit, a little higher up, a palace for himself.

So here we were enjoying the sunshine and the warm weather. Although not entirely reassured by our situation, we hoped for the best. "The Revolution may never get here," Father said hopefully.

Judging from outward appearances, Father was right. The

Revolution had not yet caught up with Gagry. The town was too remote, its population of artisans and small merchants too provincial to keep pace with political developments in the far-off Capital. Even after the Bolshevik takeover in the cities, there had been no arrests in Gagry and no searches. The town's Soviet was made up of local people who wouldn't think of bothering anybody.

Just before Christmas, relatives of the Oldenburgs, Count Zarnekau and his wife, arrived in Gagry and moved into the apartment above us. Like us, they were seeking refuge from the Revolution. To celebrate the New Year 1918 they gave a midnight supper in the large banquet hall of the palace. The display of sabres and antique guns on the wall was decorated for the occasion with flowers. The long banquet table, set for fifty, was festive with ruby goblets, silver epergnes, and handsome English china. I marvelled that our host had been able to procure legs of lamb, hams, and local delicacies for the party.

The guests included army officers and other acquaintances of the Zarnekaus who happened to be staying at the nearby hotel, among them a well-known tennis player. Other guests included local dignitaries, the priest, and chief of police. Nils and I were pleased to be invited.

During the supper each guest rose in turn, made a short speech, proposed a toast, and then, following an old Caucasian custom, drained a hunting horn brimful of wine. Toasts were proposed to the Tsar, the Empress, the Tsarevich, the Russian army. At that time the Imperial family was in Tobolsk, Siberia, captives of the Bolshevik regime. One of the guests, a member of the former Duma, made a speech that went on and on until our host seized a moment's pause to compliment him on his eloquence.

This was my first adult party—I was fifteen—and I was thoroughly enjoying the delicious food and wine. That is until

I realized that soon would come my turn to make a toast and drain the drinking horn. I don't know which of the two prospects was more alarming. Fortunately our host, realizing my dilemma, saw to it that when the horn reached me it was only half full. I managed to make a brief speech about how pleasant it was to be in Gagry. I toasted the New Year and what it would bring to us all. Looking back on this occasion I am appalled to think that probably not one of all these people realized that a complete break with their past had already occurred, making them all outcasts.

January passed quietly, except that a destroyer of the Russian navy, taken over by mutineers, anchored briefly near the town's jetty. Loaded with sugar stolen from an army depot farther south, it was proceeding up the coast, selling the already scarce sugar as it went along.

Then February came and with it rumors of searches and arrests in larger towns along the coast. By then, we had been in Gagry about three months, unaffected by events elsewhere. But Father feared that sooner or later the Revolution would reach us even there. As if to confirm Father's fears, word came that civil war had broken out in southern Russia. We were completely cut off from Petrograd and from Father's bank. About that time, letters stopped coming and telegrams could no longer be sent to the Capital.

To get news of Georges, Father sent his orderly by boat to Tuapse, the nearby railroad terminal. From there he was to go by rail to Petrograd. Fedyushkin departed, but then he simply vanished. We never saw nor heard of him again. Word got through later, however, that Georges was still in our apartment on Mokhovaya Street and safe for the time being.

All these events made us uneasy. And there were rumors that the Abkhazians were getting restless. They were a fierce people who lived in mountain villages inland from Gagry.

They claimed the area as their territory, and there was even talk that they might attack the Soviet intruders someday and push them out. When Gagry's only bank closed, Father concluded that Gagry had become a dangerous trap. "We must get out of here," he said, "and the quicker the better." How to do it was the question.

Gagry *was* a trap. The coastal railroad, though only partly completed, had been dynamited. Bandits blocked the highway. The mountains were impassable. Our only possible escape was by sea, but by that route, too, escape seemed doubtful. No passenger steamers had been seen all winter. Troopships and cargo vessels passed far out at sea. Of the small craft, none had survived a recent gale. Only rowboats remained; trying to escape in one of these was hazardous. Still, something had to be attempted. We all puzzled about what to do and talked it over together.

We were at breakfast one morning. Father had just started serving the honey. He had been able to locate a jugful in the local market and had brought it home triumphantly. Honey was our substitute for butter.

All of a sudden from the town square below we heard shouting, rifle shots, and the sound of horses' hoofs.

Father rose from the table and went quickly to the balcony. We crowded behind him to get a look.

We could see people running in every direction. About fifty riders were galloping around the square. They wore fur hats and long Cossack tunics, and carried daggers in their belts. They fired their rifles into the air and shouted as they rode. The scene was one of great confusion.

"The Abkhazians!" Father exclaimed. He went back indoors to get his field glasses. Peering through them at the square, he called out to us, "It's the Abkhazians, all right. What can they be up to?" He put down his field glasses, turned to us and said, "I have to tell you that last night I heard a rumor that Bolshevik destroyers are in these waters. A landing party is all they'll need to push these wild men back into the hills."

"Destroyers?" Mother asked.

"Won't this palace be one of their first targets?" Nils wanted to know.

"Yes," Father agreed, "we must get out of here at once. There's a villa down the road. I'll go over there right now and see if we can get some rooms in it. Meanwhile, you all get ready to move." And we did. More and more we were learning to trust Father's ingenuity to get us out of danger.

It was fortunate that he was able to get us to the villa that afternoon. Early next morning, two destroyers appeared on the horizon, trailing clouds of black smoke. They came quite close to Gagry and opened fire. From the villa on the nearby hillside we watched the palace, half expecting it to crumble before our eyes.

Nothing happened. After an initial salvo—perhaps merely a warning—the destroyers lowered boats and put three landing parties on shore. There followed much shouting and gunfire near the square. The Abkhazians galloped off into the hills. The sailors soon occupied the palace.

Even so, sailors or no sailors, I couldn't resist the temptation to go back to the billiard room at the palace. Providentially, I had taken with me the key to the back door. That afternoon I made my way through the palace garden. As I entered the billiard room, I heard drunken voices. Several Soviet sailors were playing pool, much too absorbed to pay me any mind or question who I was. I noticed they were playing for money. After a while I asked if I might join the game. They weren't playing very well, and so I had no difficulty winning twenty-five rubles. They paid straight away. A second game netted another twenty rubles. And then I thought it prudent not to try my luck any further, and quietly left as I had come.

That evening a group of sailors came to our villa searching

for firearms. Father had anticipated their arrival by removing a small but crucial inner part of his service revolver. When they left, he was jubilant at having outwitted them. The gun that they had confiscated was a useless weapon.

When we got up next morning, the destroyers had gone. Again the sea was empty, and everything quiet. So far as one could tell, there was no indication that anything at all had happened. But as we again sat around a table and watched Father dole out the breakfast honey, we sensed that the events of the previous day were weighing on his mind. He was unusually preoccupied. As it turned out, he was evolving a plan. He pushed the honey jar to one side and said, "This plan of mine has got to work." He looked at each of us solemnly. "There is no other way. I am proposing that we watch the sea. Watch systematically . . . taking turns every day . . . sitting on the balcony . . . each one of us. Meantime, we'll pack and be all ready. I'll see Kalushkin, the grocer, about an exit visa. He can arrange it. . . . he knows the Soviet people well. Of course, I'll make it worth his while. Yes, and I'll tip some fishermen to have a rowboat ready. We'll get a handcart to carry our luggage. Then we'll just wait. Sit on our suitcases, ready to go. And when a steamer comes along . . ."

We waited for three weeks. Then one day, smoke appeared on the horizon. "A boat! A boat!" Nils shouted. "I see a boat!"

"I'm coming," Father called to him, reaching for his field glasses. He peered through them intently. "It's a tramp steamer," he announced. "It may be heading in our direction."

"It may not stop here," I thought aloud.

"Maybe and maybe not," Father answered. "In any case, we must be ready."

As it turned out, the steamer anchored a quarter of a mile

offshore. A launch was lowered, and we could see some
sailors manning it. Presently they headed toward the jetty.
We saw our opportunity and acted fast.

Some of what happened next is blotted from my memory.
Yet, it's clear to me what must have taken place. We hastened
down the road toward the beach, pulling the handcart with
the luggage. The fishermen were waiting with their boat. We
climbed in. They rowed us to the ship. We clambered up the
ship's ladder. That part must have been hard for Mother and
Emilia. I carried Bullo. Behind us, came the two fishermen
bringing our suitcases. When Father paid them off, they
tipped their hats and disappeared down the ladder again.

Soon a launch came alongside. In it were the crew members
who had gone ashore. They climbed on board. Ten minutes
later, the ship weighed anchor and we were under way. I well
remember Gagry disappearing into the distance as I stood on
the deck of the boat. We had lived there five months. "God
was with us," Father said, "and we can all be thankful." And
we were.

We now realized for the first time that the ship was
crowded with people. Everywhere we looked, it was
packed—people squatting on blankets or sitting on suitcases
and cardboard boxes. Many spoke a language strange to our
ears. Father figured that these fellow passengers must be
Armenians fleeing from somewhere farther south. Also on
board were many soldiers, their uniforms tattered; some wore
red armbands. "They must be deserters," Father commented,
"from the Turkish front."

"Please go and find the purser," Mother said to Nils. "Ask
him if we can have a cabin."

Nils was soon back. He couldn't wait to tell us: there was
no purser nor any other officer on board. . . . Below deck,
conditions were chaotic; there wasn't even one inch of
space. . . . Everybody, no doubt, was traveling without a tick-

et. . . . Nobody had any idea where we were heading. . . .

One of the crew members came by, and Nils asked him where we were going. The man spat over the rail and answered, "You can see for yourself. If the coast lies to starboard, you got to be heading north!"

"Well, in that case," Father commented, "we might as well make ourselves comfortable, and have something to eat—the chicken and the hard-boiled eggs. What else did we bring with us, Emilia?"

"Ham," Emilia answered. She was not talkative. and spoke tersely.

"Oh, yes, the ham. By all means, let's have the ham."

Father settled himself on one of the ship's skylights and we followed his example. If we were heading north, well, that was fine. That was the general direction that led back to our home in Petrograd. By the time we got there, the Bolsheviks would surely have been overthrown, we thought.

By then the sun was going down. The sea was calm, the weather quite mild. I curled up near one of the ship's ventilators, which kept me warm, and I was soon asleep.

Next morning we neared Novorossiysk, known as the Windy City because it was swept once in a while by winds of near-hurricane force. Located on the Black Sea in the northwestern Caucasus where the main Caucasus Range began, it had been the home port of the Imperial Black Sea Fleet. Fortunately, that morning the weather was good. Father had been up early, scouting around. "I've found a stoker," he reported. "He tells me there's been a mutiny in the port not so long ago. It spread through the entire fleet. Many naval officers were dumped into the sea. . . ."

"How dreadful!" Mother exclaimed.

"And the town is now run by a high-handed gang of sailors. There are sentries all over. . . . Anyone entering has his hands examined. . . ."

"Why? What in the world for?" Mother asked.

"To prove he's a worker. If so, he has calloused hands. If not . . ."

"And you believe all this?"

"The stoker had no reason to mislead me."

"Do you mean we can't land here?"

Father didn't seem to hear the question. With eyes shielded, he was examining the harbor. I followed his gaze to the pier we were approaching. There, not more than a few hundred feet from where our ship was maneuvering to dock, was another steamer. "It's about to depart," Father exclaimed. He added in a lower voice, "This may be our one chance to get out of here! Our one chance!"

When the gangplank was put down, the soldiers and refugees all rushed to get off. We watched, clutching our suitcases. Then, when the crowd had thinned, at a sign from Father, we hastened down ourselves, hurried across the pier, and stumbled up the gangplank of the other steamer. Nobody challenged us or asked Father for his papers or tickets. I was delayed in getting on because I had to stop to let Bullo do his business. As I rushed toward the ship, a sailor was leaning from the bridge, shouting at somebody to hurry. At the same time, two other sailors were getting ready to pull up the gangplank. Bullo and I made it just in time. The engines started up, the whistle blew, and we were off. Where to? We did not know.

And so began another phase of our journey. We found ourselves more comfortable. The ship was larger and less crowded. There were fewer refugees and fewer soldiers. We came upon the officers' mess. It was empty—there seemed to be no officers on board—so we settled in there. Emilia found some food in the galley, and Nils helped her to bring us hot soup. When we had eaten, we went on deck for some fresh air. There a surprise awaited us.

Loud, drunken voices came to us from the bridge. A quarrel was going on. Somebody swore and a deep voice proclaimed that if "one of those s.o.b. German submarines dared to show up," he'd "blast the Goddamn thing right out of the sea." Russia was still at war with Germany.

Two other voices on the bridge, earnest and insistent, were arguing about the ship's course. As we picked up the thread, it became clear that there was a disagreement between the soldiers and the crew. The soldiers wanted to sail north, beach the ship somewhere in the Crimea, and head for home. The crew agreed to that, but first they wanted to sail south to rifle an unguarded army depot. The argument became more intense. By then, we were well out to sea. Suddenly, the ship changed course; its bow was turning south. There was an outcry from the soldiers. They raised their guns and pointed them at the bridge. The soldiers outnumbered the crew ten to one. They threatened to shoot the crew or throw them overboard. After a while, the soldiers won out. The ship again turned north. The soldiers set up a watch on the bridge to thwart any double-dealing by the crew.

So much had been going on that nobody noticed us. Once the argument had ended, however, it was time to make ourselves scarce. We quietly slipped back into the cabin.

When I woke up next morning, the ship was rocking gently, apparently at anchor. The sun was rising and everything was still. Presumably everyone on board was asleep. I dressed and hurried up the companionway. On deck I found Father scanning the sea. Due north of us, land was faintly visible. "That must be the Crimea," Father said.

"But why aren't we moving?"

Father shrugged. "It would be my guess that the mariners of this boat don't know how to pilot us through the mine fields."

We lay at anchor all that day and through the night. Early

the next morning, out of a bank of fog, a ship appeared off our portside. A modern cargo vessel, it sailed at a steady clip, as if the captain knew what he was about. When the ship came closer, we heard excited voices on our bridge. The engines started up, we heaved anchor, and got in line behind the other ship. When it turned left, we turned left; when it veered to the right, we followed in its wake. In this strange fashion we came to the small port of Kerch. Father told us it was the easternmost point of the Crimea, guarding the Sea of Azov.

"We're out of the trap," Father said, as we disembarked at Kerch. Through his ingenuity we had escaped from Gagry; but we were not yet out of danger.

18

BEHIND ENEMY LINES

When we got off the ship at Kerch, the town seemed deserted. Mother took Bullo on leash, and the rest of us picked up the suitcases. We all trudged along the narrow street until we came to a sign that read "*Evropa.*" It appeared to be a small hotel. The front door was securely bolted, and hung with a "Closed" sign. No amount of knocking produced any response. In the meantime, Nils had peered in through a side window and had seen a light inside. We went around and pounded on the back door. At first there was no answer. Then, finally, a man's voice said, "What do you want?" It was the innkeeper. Father talked to him through the door. It took considerable persuasion to get the man to open up. When finally he unlocked the door, he seemed extremely nervous. He was a heavy man with little darting eyes. He was alone there. His name, he said in a hoarse voice, was Gorbunov, and all his life's savings were in the hotel.

He told us that there were no authorities in town, no police; lawless elements, including quite a few army deserters, were on the loose. He seemed surprised that no one had molested us as we walked from the ship to the hotel. "You certainly are lucky," he kept saying, "lucky." The town, he said, had been ruled for a time by a local Soviet. Only the day before, the Bolsheviks had cleared out. They fled when they heard that the German army was advancing, its vanguard only eighteen miles away. He had closed his hotel just in time to keep it from being looted. We could stay the night, he said, but he had no food to offer us except black bread and cheese. We were grateful for that. Emotionally exhausted, we were ready for bed.

It didn't take the Germans long to restore order in Kerch. A proclamation appeared on every vacant wall in town. It called on the population to surrender its firearms. After twenty-four hours, it warned, anybody caught with a gun would be shot. Since it was clear the Germans meant what they said, all firearms were immediately surrendered.

As part of their new regime, the Germans introduced band concerts in the park. During the concerts, German officers promenaded back and forth in front of the bandstand as if to remind everyone they were in control.

It wasn't long before the German military police arrived at our hotel and took down our names. In this way we technically became prisoners of war. But Father acted fast: before anybody could put restrictions on our movements, he promptly called on the officer in command of the German troops at Kerch.

None of us in the family—certainly not Mother—was at all surprised when Father went to see the German commander. It was characteristic of him to look to the human side in any situation. I can now see that in the course of our escape from Gagry, and beyond, this attribute was crucial.

Presenting himself at headquarters, he asked to see the aide-de-camp of the commanding officer. When the aide appeared, Father handed him his card. The young captain looked it over carefully and then, apparently impressed by Father's rank and title, escorted him to his superior, Oberstleutnant von Tannstein, commander of the advance forces that occupied Kerch.

"Is there anything we can do, Herr General, to help you?" the commanding officer inquired. Father explained that he planned to take his family to Riga, and, since it would be necessary to travel behind the German lines, he hoped he could obtain authorization. In passing, Father mentioned that before the war he had been decorated with the Prussian Order of the Red Eagle and that, when the German crown prince visited Russia, he had served as his escort. Up to that point the German colonel had been punctiliously polite, but cool. But then he became amiable, brought out a bottle of cognac, and offered some to Father. "Of course, Your Excellency," he said. "Of course. I'll have a pass made out for you immediately."

Before we left for Riga, we went to visit Mother's cousin, Uncle Sanya Trubetzkoy, who had a small estate fifteen miles from Kerch. It was by then within German-held territory. Uncle Sanya came to fetch us in his car. When we got there, he gave Nils and me a loaf of French bread and some freshly churned butter. We immediately sat down on a tree stump and had a feast. We hadn't seen white bread or butter in a long time. Nothing ever tasted so delicious.

For Father the visit was of great importance. Uncle Sanya lent him 5000 much-needed rubles. I learned about it only years later from a letter Nils wrote Father. Nils was then on his way from Copenhagen back to southern Russia to join the White Army under General Denikin. Father had asked him to repay the loan. Nils wanted Father to know that he had tried, but had been unable to find Uncle Sanya.

A few days after our visit to Kerch, we went to the railroad station to say good-bye to Uncle Sanya. His brother, Nika, was ill in Moscow, and he felt he had to pay him a visit. The last we saw of Uncle Sanya, he was waving to us from the window of a crowded coach as the train pulled out of the railroad station. We were never able to find out what happened to him. We never even learned whether he had reached Moscow.

Soon we, too, would leave the Crimea. First we had to get from Kerch to Sevastopol, less than 150 miles to the west as the crow flies. Unfortunately, there was no direct route. Along that stretch of coast lay several estates—the Tsar's residence, Livadia, the Yusupov estate, Grand Duke Georges' Kharax which we had once visited, and others. To preserve the natural beauty of the area and to protect the estates, no railroad had been built along the coast. So we had to make our way inland around the Crimean peninsula in rickety trains, jostled together on wooden seats. German soldiers crowded every car. The few sandwiches we had brought with us from Kerch seemed too scanty fare for the long journey.

After eighteen hours of traveling, changing trains, and waiting, we reached Sevastopol. The strain had begun to tell on all of us. Father looked weary. Mother must have been weary, too, but seemed able to take the strain. Nils had long since lapsed into silence. Emilia, usually even-tempered, was grumpy and unobliging. Bullo slept. As for me, I was ravenously hungry and wondered, not about the great port we would soon see, but about the kind of food we would have when we got there.

Thanks to Father's foresight, we had been invited to stay overnight in Sevastopol at the home of a banker friend and his wife. Their villa overlooked the harbor. Refreshed by a delicious dinner, I stood on the terrace at sunset to look at the view below. Swinging peacefully at anchor, after spectacular action in the Atlantic, was the famous crusier *Goeben*, symbol of the German conquest.

How many times had Sevastopol changed hands, been fought over? "The Charge of the Light Brigade" came to mind as I gazed at the lights of the city all around the bay. I had read about the battle in school. It was only later that I learned how heroic was that charge by the British cavalry.

In Kerch Lieutenant Colonel Von Tannstein had graciously arranged for our passage by sea from Sevastopol to Odessa. Thus, the following day, we left as scheduled on a German troopship. As we came out into the open sea, a school of dolphins caught up with us and, to our delight, formed a playful escort. We watched them until dark. "A good omen, these dolphins," Father commented as we turned in for the night.

The following morning our ship came into the harbor of Odessa, an impressive sight when approached from the sea: the cargo ships loading and unloading, the activity at the waterfront, the flight of steps leading down to the harbor. It took Nils to remind us that here, in 1905, the crew of the cruiser *Potyomkin* had mutinied. He wondered how much hidden support the Bolsheviks might still have in the port city.

Father's authorization to travel behind the German lines went only as far as Odessa. To proceed to Riga via Kiev and Warsaw, he had to petition the German authorities in the Ukraine, and it took three months to get the necessary papers. In the meantime, we rented an apartment in the residential section of Odessa.

July 24, 1918, was my parents' twenty-fifth wedding anniversary. Here was an occasion to celebrate. As it happened, Uncle Misha Grabbe, Father's brother, and Aunt Sonia happened to be in Odessa at the time. They took us all to lunch. Until recently Uncle Misha had been Ataman of the Don, but he was almost as well known for his ability at bridge. Before lunch I tried to engage him in conversation about bridge in the hope of picking up a few pointers. He implied that he couldn't be bothered with amateurs like me and closed the subject. I might add that later in Paris he supported his family by playing bridge for high stakes. Incidentally, Father never let Uncle Misha know that the Tsar had first asked him to be ataman and that he had suggested his brother for the honor.

As was his custom, Uncle Misha was lavish in his entertainment. We drank Mother's and Father's health in the best champagne; and, for the occasion, he and Aunt Sonia presented my parents with two miniature silver vases, appropriately engraved. It seems to me now that their gift sustained their confidence in the world they had known as much as it honored a wedding anniversary.

During our stay in Odessa, we paid a call on the Tolstoys at their suburban villa by the sea. Mrs. Tolstoy seemed anxious. She had not heard from her husband. He was still in Bolshevik-held territory to the north, or so she believed. The daughter, Dalyetchka and son Seryozha were as friendly as in the old days when I went to their dancing class in St. Petersburg. Seeing them again brought memories of the fun we had had together as children. But where was their glamour? It had faded; they were worried and subdued. No doubt their confidence in their wealth and position had been shaken. Like our family and everyone else in the world we had known, they were groping for a new security.

In the center of Odessa was a large pool hall where, gratefully, I played for small stakes with anyone available. Usually my winnings paid for transportation and lunch.

One of the pool tables was especially large. It was used for competitions and had bleachers at one end. I wanted to play on this special table, but it always seemed to be reserved. Then one morning, I noticed a man practicing on it. He was alone. For a few minutes I watched him and judged that though he played quite well, with a little luck, I had a chance of beating him. So I walked up to the table and offered to play a game with him. He was a youngish underworld type with a broken nose, a flashy black velvet jacket and flaming red tie.

"Just one game," he said, "while I'm waiting for my friends. No more. Ten rubles will be the stake." This seemed rather high, so I got him to agree to a handicap. As we started to play, my partner's friends came in and settled themselves in the bleachers to watch our game. My partner was the better player, but I was exceptionally lucky. I even pocketed an impossible ball all the way across the table. That stroke gave me the game.

My partner was not so sure he wanted to pay me. He began to argue, claiming some technicality. At that point the men who had been watching the game came over. One of them, a hard-looking older man who must have been the leader, intervened. "You agreed to the stake, didn't you?" he said. "And now you've lost, so you pay up." My partner reluctantly produced a ten-ruble bank note.

"Here, take it," he said.

The men turned to go. As they left, I heard the older man say, "You don't take advantage of a kid! That's not the way to play the game."

Soon after this incident, we were on our way again. In Kiev we changed trains. That made it possible for Uncle Fedya and Aunt Lina Bezak to come to the railroad station to see us. They had an estate in the area. Thoughtfully they brought us a hamper of food and wine to take with us. Uncle Fedya cheered Mother with news that he had arranged to get Uncle Sasha and Uncle Kolya out of Bolshevik-held territory. General Skoropadsky, Germany's puppet head of the Ukraine, had negotiated with the Soviet Government to let one last train leave the Russian capital for Kiev. How sad it was that Uncle Kolya missed the train. Only Uncle Sasha was rescued by Uncle Fedya's efforts.

We were in Kiev barely a few hours before boarding a fast train for Warsaw. One other passenger shared our second-class compartment, a Pole bound for Vilna. He looked taciturn, and so he was, as Father discovered when he tried to converse with him. As we made our way closer to the Baltic, we noticed that Emilia's spirits picked up. She even became more talkative. If we ever got to Riga, she confided, she hoped to take a small Christmas vacation to visit her home near Tallin. She hadn't seen her family for several years. Alas! Emilia's hopes were not yet to be fulfilled. By Christmas, most of Estonia was gone. Before she could get there, Soviet troops had invaded her country.

As the German troop-line stretched from Riga to the Crimea, we were routed through Lvov. We reached Warsaw, exhausted, after thirty-six hours on the train. A cab took us to the nearest hotel, where we had supper and were glad to find beds for the night.

After one more day's journey, we reached Riga on September 3, 1918.

"Let us hope it won't be too long," Mother said, "before we'll be back home again."

From Kerch to Sevastopol to Odessa to Kiev to Warsaw we had made our way north behind enemy lines all the way to Riga. It had taken us nearly half a year to travel a distance ordinarily covered in a few days.

19

ESCAPE

When we reached Riga in September 1917, the German Army of Occupation had controlled the city for about a year. Order prevailed: the streets were swept, trains ran on time. To us the Latvian capital seemed a good stopover on our way home to Petrograd.

At that time few people anywhere realized that Communism had come to Russia to stay. The newspapers, at least those that fell into our hands on our way north, gave no clue of what was happening. They even reported the Treaty of Brest-Litovsk as a defeat for Russia. And no wonder! The Communist regime had signed away to Germany vast areas of Russia, including the Baltic states and the Ukraine. In reality, the treaty was a triumph for Lenin. It enabled him to take Russia out of the war and concentrate on fighting the anti-Communist White armies that were advancing from Siberia and from the south of Russia.

Lenin won out because he knew what the masses of the Russian people wanted and gave it to them: the soldiers wanted to go home and the peasants wanted land. His single-mindedness amounted to genius, impelled as it was by emotional fervor. His own revolutionary dedication replaced religion, and he thought it would for others. So he dared to challenge the Christian Orthodox faith that people had held for centuries.

At the time, no one could foresee the course of events. Nor could we when we came to Riga. So we moved into a furnished apartment there to wait for the fall of Communism. Yet, under the circumstances, we couldn't settle down to anything. We were all restless. Nils played Beethoven so continuously that Father started whistling snatches. Most of the time Father read detective stories. Mother took walks with two Christian Science ladies she had met. I tried to study German and algebra to qualify for the local school. Part of the time, Bullo and I explored the narrow streets in the medieval part of town, walked along the banks of the Dvina, and watched the boats come up the river from the Gulf of Riga nine miles away. In this fashion we occupied ourselves from late September through October.

Then, suddenly, on November 11, World War I came to an end. With the armistice, most of the German units guarding the city were pulled back. The city was left unprotected. At that juncture, a group of Latvian patriots headed by Karlis Ulmanis proclaimed their country's independence and appealed to the Allies for recognition and protection. The Latvians hoped the British would respond, and, fortunately for us, they did. On Armistice Day, the British government extended provisional recognition to the Ulmanis group as speaking for an independent Latvia.

Meanwhile it was reported that the Red Army had crossed the frontier of Estonia, and Riga's newspapers carried the rumor that it was turning south to Latvia. The Soviet regime wanted to insure control of bordering states.

The Bolshevik invasion of nearby Estonia made us apprehensive. Then, as the Red Army moved closer, we realized for the first time that we were in real danger. One day—it was early December 1918—a Russian neighbor, General Verigin, came and told us that the local Latvian Communists had drawn up a list of "undesirables." They were to be liquidated as soon as the Red Army entered town. We were shaken to discover that we were on the list. The question was: what could we do to get away?

The weather, I remember, had turned colder and there was lots of snow. And every day reports came in that the Red Army was moving closer to the city. From General Verigin we learned that there were nearly 40,000 German soldiers still in Riga. According to the terms of the armistice it was agreed that they would hold the advancing Red Army in check. Actually, these troops were much too demoralized to fight. There were also some Lettish regiments under Ulmanis who were already fighting to slow the Bolshevik advance; but they were ineffective, deeply divided in their loyalties. And so the Reds kept coming closer.

It was at that time, providentially, that several destroyers of the British Royal Navy steamed up the river and docked at the city pier. With them was a 5000-ton minelayer, *Princess Margaret*, converted from a Canadian-Pacific liner. As we later learned, the British had also sent some naval units to Tallin to give support to the Estonians against the Bolsheviks. They came to Riga on a similar mission—to bolster the newly formed anti-Communist government of Ulmanis.

No sooner had the British come to Riga than they sealed off part of the port with barbed wire and stationed sentries at the gates. Several recruiting stations were set up, and it appeared the British were helping the Ulmanis government to enlist the local youth for the defense of Riga.

The city was alive with rumors. Why had the British come?

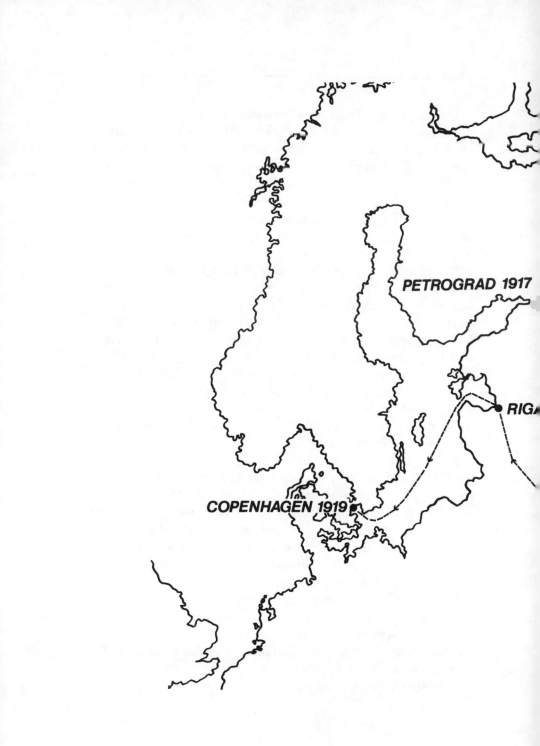

PETROGRAD 1917

RIGA

COPENHAGEN 1919

LEAVING RUSSIA
From Kerch to Sevastopol to Odessa to Kiev to Riga,
we had made our way north behind enemy lines.
It had taken us nearly half a year to travel
a distance ordinarily covered in a few days.

MOSCOW

KIEV

NOVOROSSIYSK

GAGRY

SOCHI

KERCH

ODESSA

SEVASTOPOL

Did they intend to fight? Could they prevent the Red Army from taking Riga? As if in answer to these questions, the British began drilling the local youth—or so it seemed to us. They marched the young recruits back and forth in plain view of everybody. They also took two guns off their own ships, mounted them on trucks, and staged a parade through the city. Ahead of the trucks came a band that played rousing music. Behind the trucks marched a company of British marines followed by several dozen local youth in military formation. This martial display seemed to be part of the British attempt to raise morale. Some gesture was certainly needed to reassure the population. The Red Army was only fifty miles away and closing in on Riga.

And then Father put on his navy blue serge suit and his striped red-and-blue tie and went to call on Capt. H. H. Smyth, senior officer in charge of the British ships. As he left the apartment, Father observed that he was, after all, acquainted with Admiral Beatty. He had met the famous admiral in 1914 when the Tsar entertained him in Russia. Father thought that this contact would prove helpful. It did.

There followed a day of anxious talks between Captain Smyth and Father, who had been joined by several other Russians. Captain Smyth was asked to take on board those Russian families who would be in greatest jeopardy if the Red Army entered town. He agreed, but said that persons of other nationalities had to be considered, too.

Next day Father, Mother, Emilia, Nils, and I, holding Bullo on leash, went up the gangplank of the *Princess Margaret*. We were assigned two roomy cabins, notified whom to contact in an emergency, and told where to assemble for meals. No sooner had we settled in our new quarters than a sailor knocked on the door, apologized, and said he had orders to lock all the passengers into their cabins. There was to be some action, he said vaguely.

A few minutes later, unexpectedly, our cabin shook as the British guns began to roar. Not knowing what was going on, we were startled and dismayed, and Bullo, tail down, took refuge in the closet. We presumed the shells were aimed at the approaching units of the Red Army. Locked into our cabins and unable to do anything, we didn't even know whether the Soviet troops would answer the British guns. Could the Red Army really be that close, we asked ourselves, and was it likely to be repulsed by a few shells? Father was skeptical. "What do they think they're doing?" he asked.

The bombardment by the British naval units lasted only a short time. As we learned later, it was directed at the barracks of two Lettish regiments which had mutinied and threatened to join forces with the Red Army. Once it was over, the cabins of the *Princess Margaret* were unlocked and all the passengers were asked to come to the dining salon. When we were assembled there, the captain made a brief announcement. He said that the shelling had had the desired effect. He had been assured by the Ulmanis government that no further revolt was to be expected in the city—no trouble at all as long as the British ships were there.

The passengers, Captain Smyth said, should, therefore, leave his ship. Some people pleaded with him that the Russians on board were not passengers in the ordinary sense, but refugees, and that the danger that the city would be seized by the Red Army was still very real. It was no use. The captain was adamant. "This ship is not a hotel," he said with finality. Reluctantly we all got our things together and disembarked.

Where to go? We had given up our lodgings, and somebody else had already moved in. Fortunately, General Verigin was able to return to his apartment, so he came to our rescue. He invited us to stay with him until we could make other arrangements.

The general's apartment was on the fourth floor, within

walking distance of the river. We reached it at sundown. It
had a balcony overlooking the park. After supper, Nils and I
went out on the balcony to look at the weather. It had been
snowing earlier. Outside, the cold was quite intense and the
night, dark. As we looked in the direction of the river, we
saw streaks of light crisscrossing the sky. At first we paid no
particular attention, but when the beams continued moving
back and forth across the sky, it dawned on us that they must
be floodlights from the British ships. But why? Why were
they lighting up the sky?

"They can't be looking for airplanes," said our host, who
had joined us on the balcony. "The Reds can't have enough
airplanes to risk even one. But if not planes, then what?" he
speculated. "No, no, it couldn't be! Surely they wouldn't be
signaling for us to come . . . come back on board. Unless
. . . unless they are about to sail?"

We stood there silently for a moment, too appalled to
speak. It had not even occurred to us that the British ships
might sail without us. But . . . yes, it was a possibility. We
sprang into action. Nils and I put on our coats and dashed
out to investigate.

When we reached the British sentries at the pier, Nils asked
if anything was up. One of the sailors said, "Yes, yes, we're
about to sail. Hurry! Get back on board as fast as you can!"

We ran all the way back to the general's apartment. Mother
had already gone to bed. We got her up. Hurriedly we re-
packed our suitcases and carried them downstairs. As luck
would have it, a car was passing by; Father hailed it. The
driver wanted an exorbitant amount to take us to the river.
General Verigin quickly handed him the money. Mother,
Emilia, and Bullo got into the car. We piled our suitcases in
the back. In another minute the car was off. Father, the general, Nils, and I followed on foot, half walking, half running
toward the river. The street was very slippery. The snow had

started up again and the flakes fell heavily, muffling all sound. We couldn't see more than half a block ahead of us.

When we reached the *Princess Margaret* we were shown to the same cabins we had occupied that morning. On board we noticed new faces among the passengers. Apparently not all the earlier group of Russians had seen the lights in the sky, while other people had seen the signaling, guessed its meaning, and managed to get on board. Among these others were quite a few Letts, several Estonians, and even a French family. We heard one of them remark that the *Princess Margaret* and the destroyers were leaving because the Bolshevik fleet was reported to have sailed out of Kronstadt to intercept the British in the Gulf of Riga. I heard the Frenchman say to his wife, "What will become of those young men the British have recruited if they are left behind?" And what about the Russians left behind? I wondered. Somebody else observed that it was fortunate the river had not yet frozen over, so we could get away.

There was another, overriding reason for the withdrawal of the British warships from Riga. As we learned later, Captain Smyth had been trying to get the German General von Esdorff to rally his troops and stem the Bolshevik advance. But the Germans, it appeared, had no intention of abiding by the terms of the armistice. Instead of fighting, they planned to evacuate all of Latvia, even abandoning their stores and weapons. Thus, at the eleventh hour—as the Bolshevik army had come within twenty-five miles of Riga—it became clear to Captain Smyth that the Germans would not defend the city. Realizing that the naval units under his command could not do so all by themselves, he had no alternative but to order his forces to withdraw.

And so, an hour before dawn on January 3, 1919, the British ships cast off from their moorings and sailed down the river, single file. First came the destroyer *Valkyrie*, then the other destroyers, and finally our ship, the *Princess Margaret*. As we got under way, I stood near the rail and watched the city fade in the eerie winter light. Soon there were only snow-covered banks on either side, barren and desolate.

It had stopped snowing and the moon was still out, low in the west. Occasionally I heard a rifle shot. It seemed to come from the right bank. We traveled the nine miles to the Gulf of Riga in complete silence, gliding, ghostlike, through the murky waters of the river. Once in the open sea we set our course to the northwest.

Two days later we reached Copenhagen. As we entered port, we heard the news that the Bolsheviks had taken Riga.

Before we disembarked, Father, General Verigin and several others took up a collection among the passengers so we might give some token of our gratitude to our British rescuers. Several Russians went ashore to a jeweler, bought a silver epergne, and had an inscription engraved on it. The following day a presentation was made on board the *Princess Margaret*. During the ceremony, one of the Russians who spoke English well read aloud the inscription on the silver bowl: "Four hundred refugees of all nationalities assembled in Riga will always retain a grateful memory of their deliverance from the Bolsheviks in January 1919 by the gallant captain of H.M.S. *Princess Margaret*, officers and men."

Captain Smyth accepted the epergne in the name of the British government. He thanked the passengers and said that he would take the gift to England, where it would be placed on permanent display.

Years later I learned that the epergne had indeed been designated "Naval Trophy P 377" and had been placed in the wardroom of H.M.S. *Sultan* at Gosport near Portsmouth, England. In May 1976, I myself saw it there. A friendly officer of the day opened the display cabinet and handed me the handsome piece.

"It's beautiful," he said. "On festive occasions we bring it out and use it as the centerpiece on our table, filled with flowers." I held the *epergne* in my hands and again read the words: "Four hundred refugees . . ."

"I was one of them," I said with some wonder that it had all happened to me.

When our family landed in Copenhagen we didn't know that we had left Russia forever. All of us except Nils. He would return to Russia to fight and die in the White Army.

During World War II, Mother and Father came to New York from Monte Carlo, where they had been living, America became a haven for them. After many years of precarious status as refugees, they were pleased to become US citizens. Father died at eighty-two, content in the thought that a grandson would soon be born. Mother also died at eighty-two, five years later. She, too, is buried on the bank of the Housatonic River in Connecticut near the clump of birch trees she so admired. Only Nils returned to the Russian earth.